FRIENDS OF FIELDWORKERS:
TRUE PERSONAL STORIES OF TRIUMPHS, TEARS AND INVISIBILITY

12-17-19

Dear Tammy Duckworth -
Your quote about why it's important to have women in politics was never truer than it is today.

FRIENDS OF FIELDWORKERS:

Thank you!
Judy

TRUE PERSONAL STORIES OF TRIUMPHS, TEARS AND INVISIBILITY

A Chronicle of Love

JUDY FISK LUCAS

Judy Fisk Lucas

A Spanish, full-color version will be available soon

Photo on cover: *Running Woman*, by Roxie Ray, www.RoxieRay.com

Print information available on the last page.

Rev. date: 09/21/2019

To order additional copies of this book, contact:
Xlibris
1-888-795-4274
www.Xlibris.com
Orders@Xlibris.com
789476

Told by Judy Fisk Lucas
Paintings by Roxie Ray
Photos by Judy or Ted Lucas unless specified
Edited by Ted Lucas

JFL: Dedicated to all fieldworkers and their families we know and hope to know in the future; and to Margo (Susan) Geiger, a passionate supporter, who died unexpectedly on May 4, 2019.

TDL: To those loyal helpers, Alma, Patricia and Roanna, who respond to our calls for assistance without hesitation.

RR: My paintings are dedicated to the invisible in our midst—industrious and irreplaceable—and bringing them into the light.

CONTENTS

LEVEL 1

LEVEL 2

LEVEL 3

LEVEL 4

LEVEL 5

LEVEL 6

LEVEL 7

PART II

PART III

PART IV

PART V

PART VI

FOREWORDS

From supporters of Friends of Fieldworkers:

Farm workers are the backbone of our local and global food systems. We would not see nourishing, whole foods in our grocery stores or at our farmers' markets if it weren't for the hard work of our fieldworker brothers and sisters. Because of their skilled service to our community, we are able to feed our families every day. Judy and Ted Lucas, co-founders of Friends of Fieldworkers, Inc., created an organization that lives into a spirit of relational reciprocity by directly supporting these fieldworker families. Their organization provides assistance with healthcare, childcare, education and housing. Through the work of Friends of Fieldworkers, Inc., we see that the human family is an interdependent web of relationships in which we are all called to serve and care for one another.

-Alise Echele (School Nutrition and Garden Educator)

Having worked with Cesar Chavez and other farmworkers in the labor movement, I want to thank you for what you've been doing for the past several years for the hardworking and often forgotten agricultural workers in Ventura County. Thank you, too, for being a model for others who might care about fieldworkers but not know how to show them or what to do.

-Lupe Anguiano (Community Volunteer)

TESTIMONIALS BY FIELDWORKERS

For: Judy and Ted. Thanks for being a part of my life.

I wanted to say Happy Mother's Day on Sunday and thank you for all you've done for us. When you guys helped me read and put money in my education bank account. And gave me stuff like shirts and pants and toys and books. It makes me feel happy because I have everything, thanks to you.

–M.P. (9 years old)

Thank you so much for caring about us! My dream is to have my documents one day and live here legally with my family.

–J.H.

In these moments my mother who is sick is on my mind all the time... My dream is to see her again, but I see that may almost be impossible...I can go...but I am also afraid I will not find a job over there. And I probably can't come back. It is difficult. It is very difficult.

–V.R.

How is your family? My dream is to work in a "normal" job, not in the fields. Also, to spend more time with my family and my children. And maybe to live in another place someday.

–R.D.

Thank you for thinking about us and supporting us. My dream is to stay in this country...

–S.D.

I try to work hard to raise my children. Since I met you, I feel blessed to know you. I hope God provides health so you may live many, many years. My dream, more than anything, is to not lose my job and to continue raising my children so one day they don't struggle as much as I did... and they may have an education.

–R.R.

We're so grateful for Friends of Fieldworkers, for every help that you guys did for us. I hope God bless you and your work. And God bless FOF forever and I want to say thank you, God, for meeting Judy and Ted Lucas. Both are for me, my family. I hope God gives more to FOF so they can help many more people who need help.

–P.V.

Friends of Fieldworkers has helped us a lot. They give us about half of our food right now because we don't earn a lot of money by working in the fields. Every time FOF helps us, it makes us happy a lot, especially my kids. And having new friends is helping us a lot. We feel happy and I don't worry as much because we have helpers who help us.

It has changed how we feel about working in the US. There are not many jobs where we come from. I would earn $25 a day for working 12 hours in the fields. If we got sick, we didn't get paid but here we do have some sick leave. FOF has given us some things we didn't have before—enough diapers, wipes, toys, and clothes. Before, we sometimes went to churches and asked for help. Now they call or come to us to make sure we are o.k.

Judy and Ted helped us when my children were in the hospital at different times. I feel very proud of Judy and Ted. They feel like my second mom and dad. We're all human but we are also different. We are Mexican and they are born here. There's not many who help us.

We are happy for any way FOF can help us. Our future has changed because of them. We don't worry about what's going to happen next week like we used to. Now we have hope and friends to help us. Our children feel like they have a second grandma and grandpa because their other ones are in Mexico and they probably will never meet them. Every time they see Judy and Ted, my kids are happy a lot. I feel very happy, too. My children run to the van and call them, "Abuelita! Abuelo!"

–R.A. & J.A.

COMMENTS BY SUPPORTERS OF FRIENDS OF FIELDWORKERS

Friends of Fieldworkers is a genuine heart-felt charity. Each time I donate to them I know it is going to a good cause. Makes my heart feel joy thinking of all the love Judy puts into the fieldworkers, helping them have a better life. I really appreciate Judy and Ted and know their hearts are in the right place.

–K.D. (Movie maker)

To me, Friends of Farmworkers represents the light we yearn for during these dark times. It is proof that with love and compassion for one another, we can inspire others and make this world a better place.

–A.R. (Student and FoF Board member)

I am so impressed with the way in which Friends of Fieldworkers continues to support and better the lives of fieldworkers who need an extra hand from time to time. I read and hear about how children and young people, in particular, are helped in a way that their future is more hopeful.

–A.G. (International Church Planter, FoF consultant)

Friends of Fieldworkers represents to me, love in action. When one human being insists that reaching out to neighbors in need, does not require endless discussions and committees, and only requires care and determination, then you get Friends of Fieldworkers.

Judy Lucas wanted to help fieldworker families whose homes were destroyed in a fire. She responded immediately and has continued to find ways to support those families. She has been transformed in the process and given a lot of us opportunities for transformation as well. Friends of Fieldworkers is what happens when action comes before words. Thanks be to God for it!

–J.M. (Priest)

I discovered Friends of Fieldworkers one day when researching organizations that support families that may not be able to receive assistance from government organizations. As a social worker in a pediatric medical clinic primarily serving low-income families, I see the impact that poverty can have on a child's medical and mental health. Friends of Fieldworkers has been such a blessing to many families at our clinic. We see many families where one or both of the parents work in the fields. Often, they are large families living in one small room. On top of that, many of the families have a child with chronic medical needs. Friends of Fieldworkers has provided financial and emotional support for many of these families in the form of groceries, meals, furniture and more. We at Pediatric Diagnostic Center are very grateful for Judy and everyone at Friends of Fieldworkers.

–A.L.C. (Social worker)

FoF brings together the important work of raising awareness and meeting physical needs. The Lucas' deep care and concern for many farm worker families is reflected in the intentional and long-lasting relationships they develop, as well as their commitment to making sure others know about the unjust plight their fellow neighbors experience on a daily basis.

–S. N. (Farm Administrator)

Friends of Fieldworkers is one of my favorite nonprofits because when I give to them, I know that the funds are going directly to people who are local and often overlooked. FoF blesses me with updates on the families and it makes me feel more connected to them. Very few nonprofits excel at what FoF has done and in such a short amount of time.

–C.H. (Mom, Home School Teacher, Business Owner)

A LETTER TO OUR READERS

In the middle of the afternoon on October 27, 2013, a fire blazed through the homes of twenty-seven families in Oxnard, California. Most of them were fieldworkers. What wasn't burned was stolen by looters. The Red Cross put families up in Oxnard College gymnasium and then in a local elementary school.

Living among coffee farmers since childhood in Kona, Hawaii, and starting my teaching career in Soledad and Chualar, California, with migrant children, I've always cared deeply for farmworkers. When I heard about this fire, I couldn't stay away from the burn site. I scouted through the remains of people's homes and was horrified to see blackened palm trees, gutted and mutilated structures of single-wide trailers, and skeletons of rat-infested apartments that should have been razed years ago. But these were homes to moms and dads with children—including a newborn—to elders, and to their beloved pets. All their earthly possessions were gone. One woman, the daughter of a minister, was raising money for art supplies for her church's children. She kept the $137.46 in a coffee can in her closet. It was gone. Several people lost their rent money that was kept in their homes until the first of the month.

I saw twisted, blackened toys, backpacks and clothes. Tiny gardens beside some of the homes had charred vines with tiny red cherry tomatoes still attached. And then I saw something that changed everything for me: a charred tricycle locked to a random pipe sticking out of the ground. *Why on earth would a toddler's trike have to be chained up anyway?*

The Red Cross helped the fire victims through the first 6-8 weeks with shelter, food, clothing, and other necessities. I couldn't imagine trying to put my little ones to sleep on cots, in a gymnasium, mere feet away from others. And then laying there in the semi-dark, wondering where I would live and how I would care for my family after this.

The Red Cross organizers, moved by the peaceful, polite and gracious orderliness of the fire victims, mostly from the Mexican state of Oaxaca, worked with them longer than usual, assisting them to find available apartments—scarce and expensive—and providing vouchers for the first month's rent, beds and some other necessities.

There are more than 20,000 indigenous people in Ventura County, mostly from the Mexican states of Oaxaca, Guerrero and Puebla, who are coming in greater numbers to Oxnard to work in the fields. And thank goodness. Without them, our agricultural industry would collapse.

I went to a community meeting where I met many of the fire victims, including children, and invited them to share their needs with us. My husband, Ted, and I were hooked. These people had certain qualities that endeared them to us immediately. Their strength, courage, politeness, kindness, faith and love of family where striking. Even the fire fighters and Red Cross workers were touched by these families and said so.

That's when Friends of Fieldworkers began. And in May, 2015, it was incorporated as a nonprofit charity to meet the continuing needs of about twelve extended families from the initial fire and more people we met. Food, clothing, shoes, books, furniture, and other household items were not the only things we were able to provide. We wanted to develop long-term and meaningful friendships with fieldworkers.

We cannot and have not done this work alone. Almost weekly, we learn of more needs of farmworkers through the referrals of agencies, churches, and other fieldworkers. Our fundraising is primarily done by asking our family, friends, churches and other organizations for money and specific items. Support does come from unexpected places.

We meet potential volunteers in our daily path. They often ask, "How does Friends of Fieldworkers work? What can I do?" That's how this book came to be.

An early supporter of Friends of Fieldworkers (FoF), personal friend, and co-founder of Studio Channel Island is Roxie Ray. She has observed and painted fieldworkers for many years. We met her in 2000 at Studio Channel Islands when it was housed on the grounds of the future California State University Channel Islands, before it opened its doors to students. Friends of Fieldworkers' co-founder Ted Lucas drove every day on University Drive to the new campus, bordered by strawberry fields tended by fieldworkers.

Do you see me? by Roxie Ray, www.RoxieRay.com

The CSU Channel Islands founding president Handel Evans and his wife, Carol, made it possible for the artists of Studio Channel Islands to have their first home in one of the abandoned buildings, formerly a part of Camarillo State Mental Hospital. After much volunteer work on the cold, abandoned space, the art studio became a center of life, light and creative energy before the university actually opened its doors to students.

As the wife of Ted Lucas, who would eventually become California State University Channel Islands' first Vice President for Academic Affairs and Provost, I loved wandering around the old hospital grounds, discovering the sights and sounds of this historical site that housed over 7,000 patients at its peak. That's when I met Roxie and saw her paintings of fieldworkers—twenty years ago. I was mesmerized by Roxie's capture of the essence of fieldworkers on canvas. We have talked many times over the past two decades about collaborating on a project to highlight one of our state's most valuable and often unrecognized treasures: the people who work in the fields.

The more I learn of the value of fieldworkers to our community, culture and economy, the more I believe they deserve our attention, respect and action on their behalf.

From the House Farm Workers! website we read:

> *Farm workers are the backbone of Ventura County agriculture. Ventura County's farms and ranches employ nearly 36,000 men and women. These farm workers are critical to Ventura County's $2 billion-a-year agricultural industry. Without them, crops would not be harvested, and the lush local landscape of green fields and orchards would go untended.*
>
> *A combination of low wages and high housing costs means farm workers often must pool their resources to live in overcrowded apartments, motel rooms or houses. Sometimes they live in garages or sheds, neither intended nor fit for human habitation.*

So now, Dear Reader, this is how you can become a friend of fieldworkers: to see, understand, befriend, love and support them. To make a difference in the lives of their families and to help make their dreams come true: to help their children succeed in America—to live, study, work and be happy, resourceful, successful and productive citizens.

Farmworkers from Mexico and other countries in Central and South America did not come to California on a whim. They weighed their options and decided that the risk was worth the possible reward.

Fieldworkers have rich and diverse backgrounds—languages, stories, customs, beliefs, close family relationships, and cultural norms. They left these behind, knowing that once in America, they would probably never be able to go back to their homeland and families because of the complicated and decades-long immigration process which would allow them in but not out of Mexico.

As one young teen told me, *Not everyone who left Mexico with us made it here. Some died in the desert or were captured and sent back.*

Why would families risk everything to come here? For life. For their children. For the hope that if they persisted long enough and hard enough, their prayers and work would pay off. Their children would not have to suffer as they have. And they would be able to send money home to their families in Mexico for food, medical bills and other basic necessities. Extreme conditions call for extreme measures.

In our present political climate, immigrants from poor countries are not wanted. They are needed. But not wanted. We are told untruths that they will take our jobs. They will bring crime. They will intermarry and dilute our culture.

None of this is further from the truth. They work jobs no one else will do. They do not bring higher crime rates. In fact, their desire to live under the radar of American surveillance makes them model citizens. And, as I see it, any intermingling of races brings a deepening of beauty, tradition, understanding and strength to the texture of our American fabric.

Any group of people that is systematically isolated, ignored, maligned or otherwise treated unfairly, even cruelly, deserves our respect, love, support, and admiration. And this can only be done though reciprocity and friendship.

And this is our story of becoming involved with fieldworkers. For the survival and success of farming and those we depend on—fieldworkers. And for the survival and achievement of the American Dream for all of us.

Peace to you always,
Judy Fisk Lucas & Ted D. Lucas

OUR MISSION

First and foremost, our mission is to become friends of fieldworkers. And we want to support them on their journey from surviving to thriving.

The following are some things that we have done, are doing now or we dream of doing for fieldworkers. Some activities we have done hundreds of times such as providing clothing and shoes. Some, we have only done once or twice, such as the Mother's Care ASAP and Santa Barbara Zoo visit. And, the things we want to do but haven't yet, are written in magic marker on paper charts taped up around our house.

Nearly every day I start the day with a yellow legal pad, lined to make four boxes and labeled: DO, GO, CALL/TEXT, WRITE/ EMAIL. Then I fill in the boxes as I remember things to do and get physical pleasure when I cross them off. My mother introduced me to that technique.

As a retired teacher, I am a huge fan of Abraham Maslow and although I did not *plan* to design our Friends of Fieldworker program based on his Hierarchy of Needs, I was pleasantly surprised to learn that most of what we have done over the years can roughly be fit into 7 categories. He started out with five, then added six, seven and eight categories. I found one through seven to be most useful as a visual for the types of things we do. And so, you will notice that according to his pyramid, the first level of human needs and the largest, has the most activities.

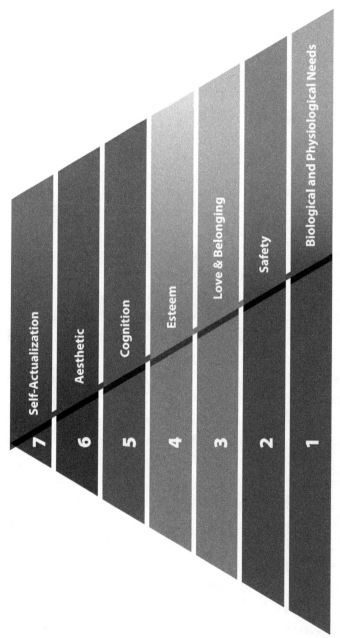

Maslow's Pyramid of Basic Needs

7 Self-Actualization
6 Aesthetic
5 Cognition
4 Esteem
3 Love & Belonging
2 Safety
1 Biological and Physiological Needs

Maslow's Pyramid of Basic Needs Adapted for Friends of Fieldworkers, Inc.
by Jane Shanahan, design aesthetic/by jane; www.theaestheticprinciple.com

According to Maslow, until people's most basic *physiological and biological* needs are met for air, water, food, clothing, shelter, medical and dental care, etc., they don't, as a rule, go to the next level, *safety*. And when those needs are met, they are inherently free to move to the next level. Some people are stuck at level one forever, for various reasons.

Friends of Fieldworkers, Inc., wants people to be free and supported in becoming their very best selves. And that means, going as high up that pyramid as possible, solving as many problems as possible, overcoming as many obstacles as they can. Working in the fields, growing and harvesting our food, is one of the few options they have. But hopefully, they can move from the fields into less backbreaking, dangerous and repetitive work sometime in their lives.

We have learned that for some first-generation immigrants, their highest goal is supporting their children, the second generation, to move up that pyramid. As one grandfather fieldworker described his achievement in life,

I gave up my knees for my children to go to college and succeed.

Some of the activities we describe here fit into more than one level. For example, getting orthodontic work done on children's teeth fits into 3 levels: (1) biological and physiological (medical & dental), (2) love and belonging (receiving acceptance and being part of a group) and (3) esteem (for one's self and one's appearance). A healthy smile gets respect and positive attention unconsciously. The two young women we have gotten braces for noticed immediately, a change in others' perceptions of them. This is sad but true. They smile more often. Speak more freely. Stand up straighter and radiate more self-confidence. That's our experience, anyway.

Finally, throughout this book we use the terms "fieldworker" and "farmworker" interchangeably, and "FoF" is the acronym for Friends of Fieldworkers, Inc.

The following activities are categorized under the <u>most basic level</u> of need they meet.

LEVEL 1

Biological and physiological needs: air, drink, food, shelter, warmth, sex, sleep, clothing, medical and dental care (I added the last two which seem obvious.)

1

FIRE!

Over the past six years, I have visited the sites of three fires involving farmworkers—in Port Hueneme and Oxnard, California. The first fire happened in midafternoon in a run-down collection of apartments and single trailers rented primarily to fieldworker families. The fire started in the adjacent vacant lot and swept through the ghetto in a matter of minutes. Thankfully, no lives were lost because parents were either at work or picking up their children at school. A few families went to live with relatives; the rest were housed in Oxnard College gymnasium by the American Red Cross. They moved a few weeks later into another local school gymnasium until they could find more permanent housing elsewhere.

In spite of poor water, heat and hygienic conditions in these burned homes, the families had developed friendships and a sense of community. Now every family scrambled to find a place they could afford in the cities of Ventura, Oxnard and Port Hueneme.

Finding affordable housing in Ventura County is nearly impossible. From the House Farm Workers! website I found these sobering facts: *The average income of those workers is about $22,000 a year. Yet the average apartment rent in Ventura County is more than $20,000 a year.*

Spread out as they were, families had to readjust to new communities where they didn't know anyone. Their children sometimes had to change schools. Parents had to find new ways to get to their field jobs.

Friends of Fieldworkers (yet unnamed) supplied food, clothing, shoes, bedding, dishes, small appliances, some furnishings and other necessities of daily life for about two-thirds of the families. The Salvation Army, Goodwill and St. Vincent de Paul provided beds and other items. The Red Cross supplied counseling and money for rent and other necessities in addition to all they did in the first weeks to provide shelter and food, etc.

At present (summer, 2019) we are still in touch with about twelve of those original families who have since integrated into their new communities.

In 2016, a fatal fire swept through an 8-plex apartment in Port Hueneme during the night. One young woman lost her husband and five-year-old son. They were killed after the father was able to bring her and their little daughter to safety. Seven families lost all or some of their belongings.

We had a GoFundMe campaign and raised $1,000 each for six of the households that lost the most. With the help of St. Jude's Church of the Apostles' Loaves and Fishes group, we also supplied food, water, clothing, diapers, and other items, plus moral support. The Outlaw Quilters' group provided handmade quilts. I rescued some of the victims' outdoor plants and cared for them until families had a place for them again.

Most of these tenants, having lived here for many years, had family and other resources in the area. We still connect with one of the families whose son is attending California State University Channel Islands. We have helped him pay for textbooks, which have become very expensive.

One family called two years later to invite us to their new home after they finally got resettled.

Another fire involved one family of ours who had survived the first fire. Fortunately, their apartment had only minimal smoke damage. But being awakened in the night by fire is terrifying for all. I learned from a member of the fire department that this was only one of several fires in the area that summer. Fires in marginalized neighborhoods get little or no publicity in the news unless there's a fatality. Landlords' neglect is most often, but not always, a contributing factor in these fires.

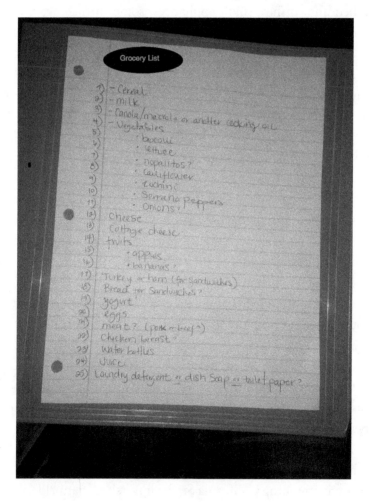

2

GROCERY LIST

When I visit families, I ask if they are low on groceries. If they tell me they are, I ask them for a list of 25 items. I go to a neighborhood grocery store that specializes in Hispanic food and particularly foods indigenous people love. Whatever is on their list, I add more of the things I know from experience that they use.

Vegetables:	chili, chayote, cilantro, onion, Poblano peppers, carrots, broccoli, lettuce, zucchini, celery, green beans and corn on the cob
Fruit:	dragon fruit, mango, guava, orange, apple, watermelon, cantaloupe, grapes and pineapple
Dairy:	whole milk, Queso Oaxaca, *Asadero* or *Quesillo*, the Mexican name for a semi-soft, white, string-type cheese made from cow's milk. Belonging to the pasta filata family and similar to a Mozzarella, Queso Oaxaca is a stretched curd cheese, kneaded and sold in long ropes gently wound in balls. *Gogurt* for the children
Dried Beans:	black, pinto, yellow, and white
Rice:	long white and vermicelli for soup
Condiments:	mayonnaise, catsup, cinnamon, oil (Safflower, Canola or olive), cumin, black and cayenne pepper
For tortilla-making:	Morton's salt (iodine) and masa flour
Meat:	ground beef, pork, turkey; stew meat; whole chicken or parts

My local grocery gives me the ends of their barbequed tri-tip (about $12.99/pound) that they can't sell. I cut up bite-sized pieces of meat, leaving some fat for flavor and make soups and stews to take to families who are under the weather. Sometimes I give all the meat to them for their own recipes. This is a delicious and nutritious meal extender.

Snacks:	popcorn, Maria Crackers and *Abuelita* chocolate tablets, syrup, or powdered mix in individual packets, made by Nestlé and used to make Mexican-style hot chocolate. (It was originally invented and commercialized in Mexico in 1939 by Fábrica de Chocolates La Azteca.)
Paper Goods:	toilet paper, paper napkins and towels, feminine napkins or tampons. Since two or more families often live together in 1- or 2-bedroom apartments, toilet paper can be a problem. Each family is expected to provide their own in the shared bathroom. Guests may need to request toilet paper. (Diapers and baby wipes are discussed in another section.)
Laundry Items:	liquid soap (without perfume or dyes), Zote bar soap, liquid or paper fabric softener, bleach, white vinegar, $10- rolls of quarters, laundry baskets, baby laundry soap if newborns are in the home
Bathroom Items:	bath soap (liquid or bars), shampoo and conditioner, toothbrushes, toothpaste, deodorant, baby shampoo if children are in the home. Bleach and disinfectant wipes are included if there's a very ill person or one with a compromised immune system in the family.
Kitchen supplies:	dish soap, white vinegar, scrubbies, dishrags and cloths, paper lunch bags, trash bags, saran wrap and foil. A special dish and pot- scrubbing Brush– Escobeta De Raiz/Root Brush– is available for about $3 at Vallarta and Tresierras Markets.

3

FOOD FORWARD

Food Forward is a local nonprofit agency that sends out volunteers to pick fruit and vegetables not needed by land owners. These are boxed up and given to other nonprofits like Friends of Fieldworkers to distribute. I try to deliver them within 2-3 days because of their perishability. I deliver the citrus and other fruit to individual fieldworker families. If a family picks raspberries, strawberries or blueberries, for example, they can bring some of them home to their families. However, they are limited to those specific kinds. Fruit in the local groceries are often picked-over, expensive and non-organic. For families to have access to freshly picked, organic, backyard fruit, is a great asset.

We live in the Ojai Valley, land of pixie tangerines, Meyer lemons, Valencia oranges, and various kinds of avocados. We are surrounded by fruit. I have asked people if I can pick from their trees. One neighbor picked the fruit himself from his prickly pear tree and gave it to me for our friends. Most are very willing to share and happy to have someone pick their fruit to prevent them from going to waste and rotting on the ground, adding to the greenhouse effect.

A few fruit tree owners refuse. Maybe they will, in fact, use all of their own fruit or share it with friends. Maybe it's that they don't approve of all the peace bumper stickers on my van.

The fruit we don't take to families in Oxnard or Port Hueneme, or send to Fillmore or Simi Valley, we sold in our own fruit stand, as mentioned later.

4

LENTIL LAVISH

There's nothing that says love or comfort better than a hot, homecooked meal. My friend Margo Geiger was an artist. She painted, sketched, crocheted and created potted succulents in a variety of containers from large Tonka Toy trucks to coffee mugs. She was also an artist in the kitchen, crafting healthy, delicious muffins for the homeless, meals for the priests of a local monastery, and casseroles and cookies for fieldworkers.

I liked to call my friend Margo when we had a family with a sick or injured family member or who was suffering some kind of loss. This recipe is one that is wholesome, delicious and economical, made for under $10. She kept everything on hand and only had to buy fresh ground beef at the Ojai Valley Ranch Market in Oak View which she swore had the best quality meat.

Lentil Skillet Bake (serves 6-8)

Ingredients:

1-quart water
1 1/2 cup rinsed lentils
1 1/2 pounds ground beef (or: 1 pound each, ground pork and beef)
2 tablespoons butter
2 medium onions, chopped
2 cloves garlic, minced
3 tablespoons long-grained white rice
1 teaspoon each, sugar, salt, and ground cumin
1/2 teaspoon ground pepper
2 tablespoons beef bouillon (or 2 cubes)
1 tablespoon cider vinegar
Parsley

Directions:

1) Bring water to boil in large saucepan.
2) Add lentils and cook, covered, for twenty minutes.
3) Drain, reserving liquid and set aside lentils.
4) To the liquid, add enough water to make 2 1/3 cups and set aside.
5) In a deep skillet, sauté onions and garlic in butter.
6) Stir in beef and brown lightly.
7) Dissolve bouillon in warm reserved liquid.
8) Add liquid to meat mixture.
9) Cover and simmer for 10 minutes.
10) Stir in reserved lentils, rice*, sugar, salt and seasonings.
11) Bring to a boil.
    Reduce heat, cover and simmer for 30 minutes or until lentils and rice are tender and the liquid is absorbed. You may add a little more water if necessary or red wine if desired.
12) Check seasonings and stir in 1 tablespoon cider vinegar. Sprinkle with parsley.

*If using brown rice, cook it first for 15-20 minutes.
Serve in an attractive casserole dish or a practical pot with lid that the family can keep.

From *More-with-Less Cookbook*, 25th Anniversary Edition by Doris Janzen Longacre. (c) 1976 Herald Press. Used with permission.

5

CINNAMON APPLESAUCE

One of my favorite crockpot recipes is applesauce. I buy a bag of apples, slightly past their prime, for 99 cents in the bargain produce section of Ojai Valley Ranch Market. I rinse them in a sink-full of water with a dash of white vinegar. I cut them into fourths, removing the core and seeds, and leaving on the peels.

I put these in the crock pot and sprinkle liberally with ground cinnamon and Chinese Five Spice or Pumpkin Pie Spice. I cover and cook on high for 2 hours. Or on low for 4-5 hours. The fragrance is intoxicating.

For smoother sauce, without peels, I run the cooked apples through a mill, like the ones used for making baby food. I may add a tablespoon of butter, but it's not necessary.

The applesauce can be frozen in small containers and thawed in the microwave when needed. I like to take them to our families as a side dish. Comfort food. Sometimes I have taken a bag of apples and a crock pot to our friends' apartments and explained the process. This is popular with the little ones.

6

CROCKPOT STEWS

These can also be made in a large pot on the stove. But I like to prepare the ingredients in the morning, put in the crockpot on low and the delectable dish is ready for dinner. (Or cook overnight.)

Beef Stew

Ingredients:

1-2 lbs. pieces of beef, cubed or cut into tiny pieces for the children
6 large potatoes (russet or sweet)
6 large carrots
1 large onion
1 bunch cilantro
1 poblano chili
1 box of beef broth (no MSG, low salt)
2 tablespoons olive oil
1 can cooked black beans
1/2 cup barley

Directions:

1. Chop up all the vegetables.
2. Brown the meat in the olive oil. (Unless the meat is already cooked such as the barbequed tri-tip ends from the deli.) This can be cut up, leaving only enough fat for flavor and added to the vegetables in the pot.
3. Mix all in crock pot and cover with water.
4. Add salt and pepper to taste. Maybe a bit of chili powder if it needs some heat.
5. Heat on high for 4 hours or low for 8 hours (or overnight).
6. Can also cook in pot on stovetop, bringing to a boil and then simmering for about 2 hours.

Chicken Stew

The only differences here are that I use chicken thighs or breast meat and chicken instead of beef broth. I also like to use white rice, macaroni or noodles instead of barley. The chicken can be cut into small pieces after cooking.

I take the stew in the original pot to a family. They will transfer it into their own pot. Or I take one I can leave. They cost $4-8 in a thrift store. I sometimes take muffins or a big loaf of bread, but they usually prefer the tortillas they make at home. Some families also use store-bought corn or flour tortillas.

7

EGGS & CHICKENS

We raise chickens here in Ojai and give eggs to families. One day I visited the home of a grandmother, mother (both widowed) and three teens. As usual, I asked the children, the most reliable on this subject, what food is needed in their kitchen.

Well, we're a little low, but we just went shopping and got some eggs.
I guessed that would be their only food for a few days. I love the idea
that our eggs are free-range, organic and hormone-free. We supplement
our hens' organic chicken food with kitchen scraps and greens from a
local cafe. We provide them with a tin bucket and exchange it with
a clean one every 3-4 days. I find free egg cartons on-line on Ojai
Unconditional Give or Take (UGOT). Our six hens provide four to
six eggs a day when laying. Eggs are an easy give. Sometimes neighbors
share their extra eggs, too. Eggs can be safely left out on the counter
for at least a month if they are fresh, kept at room temperature, and
not washed off. There is a protective enzyme on the egg shell until it's
washed off. I like to wash mine at the end of a day or two, with room
temperature soapy water and place them in the refrigerator until I have
a full carton and then deliver it in a little ice chest. I sometimes take a
children's book about chickens and eggs with me.

Kids love the antics of animals. So ours—Cinnamon, Ivory,
Lily, Goldie, Lucy and Gracie (the last four named after favorite
comediennes)—make great topics for Instagram and Snapchat. It's
a good way to stay connected with the tweens. Same for Wiley and
Willow, schnoodle and Maltipoo.

8

EATING CROW

In our country community, where it is very popular to raise
chickens for eggs, it is *not* very popular to raise roosters unless there is a
large space of land between neighbors. For this reason, there are often
announcements in the local Unconditional Give or Take (UGOT)
Internet site that "Handsome rooster needs a new home."

I discovered quite by accident that rooster meat is a delicacy for
Oaxacans. And I am always looking for new sources of protein for them.
I have one or two friends in the area, now, who are happy to pass on their
crowers to me, knowing that they will go to good homes for a special meal.

Only one time that I know of, the family fell in love with their rooster and kept him as a pet in their back yard. The father was particularly pleased with the reminder of morning music in his home village.

9

SOUP & COMPANY

One day I was struggling with a lingering flu and feeling low. I called one of my dear friends and told her how I was feeling. *What can I do?* she asked. *Would you please bring me some of your healthy, healing chicken noodle and vegetable soup?*

A couple of hours later there was a knock on my door and my friend brought her baby and young daughter from Oxnard to bring me her soup. She heated it up on the stove and watched me eat it. She told me how much she wanted me to feel better. The baby sat on the couch being entertained by our two dogs, Willow and Wiley. The nine-year-old brought a picture she had drawn that said, *Please feel better soon,* and we taped it on the cupboard where I could see it all day long. (Actually, it's still there a year later.)

I indeed did feel much better after their visit. I felt loved and cared for. My friend's parting words were, *I'll do anything for you.* So precious.

10

GINGERSNAP COOKIES

Nearly every child of Chualar School, just outside of Salinas, where I had my first teaching job in 1970, was eligible for the free meal program. Our two cooks were dedicated to the dietary health of their charges—some were the children of children they'd served over the years. The kitchen was not large, and its aromas of fresh-baking bread filled the school yard. Teachers were also invited to partake of the school breakfasts as well as the lunches.

Their gingersnap cookies were my favorite. They pared down the school-size recipe for a family-batch size and I can honestly say I've made these cookies hundreds, if not thousands, of times since 1970. Our children loved them and now our grandchildren and everyone else who eats them. Chewy, crunchy and gingery.

And so it was only natural that I'd want to share them with my fieldworker families. My friend Margo made that a new part of her holiday tradition. Last Christmas she filled ten Christmas tins with gingersnaps which we delivered to families. I also brought a little girl home with me to wrap presents and bake gingersnap cookies.

Chualar School Gingersnap Cookies

Dry Ingredients:

>2 cups unbleached flour
extra white granulated sugar
1/4 teaspoon salt
2 teaspoons soda
1 teaspoon ground cinnamon
1 teaspoon ground cloves
1 teaspoon ground ginger

Wet Ingredients:

>1/4 cup molasses
3/4 cup Crisco (or butter and coconut oil)
1 cup sugar
1 egg

Directions:

1) Sift together all dry ingredients and put in small bowl.
2) Cream together wet ingredients.

3) Mix dry ingredients into wet ingredients; mix well with electric mixer.

4) Roll dough into 1-inch balls.

5) Roll balls of dough in white granulated sugar. (I use a plastic butter tub with deep sides. Put four balls into the container with about one-inch of sugar and twirl around to evenly coat them.)

6) Place balls on an ungreased cookie pan about 2 inches apart because they spread during baking. Bake in 375 degrees oven for 10-12 minutes. Be careful not to burn them. Let cookies sit on the pan for about three minutes to cool slightly.

7) Use a spatula to transfer cookies to a cooking rack. If you flip them over, the cookies will be crunchy; if you leave them right-side-up, they will be chewy. (Or vice versa. Experiment.)

11

ORANGE PULP FICTION

Fruit juice is another topic. Our families drink mostly bottled water, apple or orange juice. The least expensive ones are Sunny D, Tropicana and other "orange drinks." And now that we have access to boxes of fruit, I like to provide electric citrus juicers along with the fruit. They can be purchased for about $16 at local drugstores and are easy enough for the children to work. I give demonstrations to those who come to my house. Once they have fresh-squeezed orange juice, they're hooked.

12

EAT-OUTS

Most of the farmworker children I have met have never eaten in a local restaurant. It is just too expensive, especially for large families. That's why I love to take them out to eat whenever possible. I'm thinking of one time we went for pizza. Another time for Thai food. Other times to Subway and In-N-Out Burger. Indian and Italian. Several times we've had snacks and drinks at Starbucks, frozen yogurt or ice cream at Baskin Robbins. (Against my better judgment of course, but so, so fun.) Each time it is a real pleasure to see them experimenting with new foods. And on other occasions they've taken us to restaurants serving Mexican and Oaxacan food. It's just one of many ways to explore each other's culture.

13

WAYWARD SOCKS

An eight-year-old Mixteco boy was rummaging through stacks of clothing on the ground. It was at a distribution of clothes, shoes, toys, bedding and other household essentials for victims of the 2013 Oxnard Fire. This little boy was earnestly looking for something, apparently without success. I asked if I could help him find some pants or shirts or a jacket. *I just need to find another sock. I can only find this one*!

That very day I started collecting new and gently used socks in all sizes. Even single socks. C.A.T. (Christians Acting Together) in Camarillo and New 2 You Thrift Store in Ojai still save socks for us, six years later. Many thrift stores do not sell used socks and are willing to save them for us when they learn what we are doing with them.

I wash all the socks, bleaching the white ones. After drying them, I toss out any with holes or stains, and fold or safety-pin the remaining pairs. I put all single socks in good condition in a bag marked, EMERGENCY SOCKS. Children often wear unmatched socks at home, anyway. Little Miss Matched Socks (c) are sold that way—sets of different patterns in the same colors!

Sometimes I put socks for all members of a family in a padded mailer and mail them at odd times in the year. Since most families don't have heat in their homes (because of the legitimate fire hazards of old and neglected wall heaters), socks are needed year-round. And unfortunately, washing machines at laundromats or at home really do consume socks.

14

CLOTHES

We get quite a few donations of clothing, food, appliances, toys, and furniture. Sometimes we've gotten as many as 20 large garbage bags at a time full of clothes. My method is to sort all of them on the garage floor.

I check items for stains, stickers, tears, other damage and inappropriate sayings and trash those.

I label containers with the following: jeans, darks, whites, towels, blankets, baby clothes, bleachables, and fine fabrics. I sort all the good clothes into those categories and put some in a Goodwill box. Some cotton clothes are cut up for clean rags which I bag separately and mark *CLEAN RAGS*.

I wash and dry the clothes and separate them into bags for individual families. Or I put them into bags labeled *men, women, children* or *infants* and store them in our garage or distribute to one of a few recipient groups: First Five Neighborhoods for Learning in various towns or Life Choices Pregnancy Clinic of Ojai Valley (a non-profit licensed medical clinic.) I also have some women who accept these clothes and distribute directly to people in need in their own communities.

15

COMFY CLOTHES

A young woman with three school-aged children suffered terribly with painful gall bladder disease. Her children called me when she was in the hospital having surgery and just before she returned home. When asked what she wanted, they said she'd really like a robe. She was unable to work in the fields during her illness and for several weeks of recovery afterwards.

When she returned home, I took Margo's Lentil Casserole for the family and a soft, comfy cotton robe and slippers for her to wear during her convalescence. I stayed long enough to say hello and give her and her family my love. Friends of Fieldworkers also provided some money toward their bills and books and toys to entertain the children during their mom's recovery.

16

MALL SHOPPING

At the beginning of her junior year in high school, a young woman, her best friend and I went to the mall together to do clothes shopping. We had a budget of $300 and found tops, pants, shoes, jewelry and even perfume. The girls tried on lots of clothes and I got to hear the joyful, giggling banter and see the fashions they chose. It was the first time my young friend had ever bought new clothes at a mall and not at secondhand stores. I asked the salespersons for special attention to them.

Together we looked for a *power outfit* that she could wear for her oral presentation the first week of school. The following week when I checked in, sure enough, she did great on her speech AND she said she felt like a WINNER!

Red Handkerchief by Roxie Ray, www.RoxieRay.com

17

TEN TOP NEEDS

I got an email from a person out of town saying he'd learned of our organization and he really wanted to help. His church was considering how they could help and wondered if certain items would be useful to farmworkers and make their jobs a bit easier. And these were items their companies did not provide.

This sounded very promising and I started putting out feelers immediately, asking people in the field and stores that supplied their needs what items where the most popular.

This is the list of the top 10 items we made, not in this order.

Rain coats, pants and hats
Cotton bandanas (3 worn at a time, multiple colors)
Boots (waterproof and sturdy with room for socks)
Cap or hat (with UV protection)
Hoodies (long-sleeved cotton/polyester blend sweats with hoods)
Igloo ice chests (medium sized)
Light colored cotton-blend socks
Water bottles
Lunch boxes with thermoses
Jackets, lightweight but warm; Patagonia has great options.

Unfortunately, I heard from this inquirer months later that they had chosen to work with another group in their community. But his first call made me consider the top ten needs and look for ways to find them.

18

LAUNDROMAT MARATHON

There have been times when the number of clothes donated made home laundering impossible. I got the help of a teenager who went with me to a local laundromat where we sorted, put the clothes in washers, added coins and laundry soap, bleach and conditioner. Then we transferred the clothes to dryers, added more quarters and folded them when dry. The clean clothes were sorted into boxes or large paper leaf bags from Ace Hardware, labeled, and put in our van.

This was a fun project to do together and it got the job done much more quickly than at home. It also enabled us to get a good look at what we were washing and folding, eliminating any clothes that weren't gently used or appropriate for fieldworkers (e.g. short midriff tops, tee shirts with scary or rude messages, dry-clean-only fabrics). Blankets, quilts, sleeping bags and other large items were much easier to manage there, too.

19

LAUNDRY LOVE

From their website with permission:

The Laundry Love initiative consists of regular opportunities to come alongside people who are struggling financially by assisting them with their laundry. Laundry love partners with groups and local laundromats in cleaning clothes and linens of low-income or no-income families and individuals. We see the laundromat as a place where strangers become friends, people are known by name, hope is hustled, and the worth of every human being is acknowledged and celebrated.

Laundry Love started in Ventura, California, in 2003. As of 2018, there are eight local chapters in Southern California and over 400 nationwide. Laundry Love seeks to encourage everyday hospitality, building trust within a community or neighborhood through human care. The chapter closest to us is supported by the St. Andrew's Episcopal Church of Ojai. There are at least four more in Ventura and several others in Ventura County. FoF has supported Ojai's program by donating money, laundry soap, conditioner and bilingual children's books for the dedicated grandma in her 80's who reads to the children while they wait for parents to finish their laundry. Many of them only speak Spanish.

Another laundry option is to fill a wine box or laundry basket with laundry supplies: liquid laundry soap and conditioner (bought on sale) and preferably with no perfumes or dyes, white cleaning vinegar, Pine-Sol and Zote, a pink bar of soap popular with Mexicans and a roll of quarters. If buying these at a dollar store, these laundry supplies (including a roll of quarters) will cost about $27.

20

UNIFORM ASSIST

Some of our students attending junior high or middle school are required to wear uniforms. On one occasion we provided funds at the beginning of the year for a teen's school uniform. It came to under $100. On another occasion we paid for a teen's basketball shoes when he was accepted on the team.

For one father working in construction, we reimbursed him on two occasions for his specialty work shoes from a local outlet store. Each pair cost $130 and lasted about a year.

On many occasions we have provided good quality tennis shoes for work. When you think about people working on their feet all day long, it is an absolute necessity that they have good shoes, possibly preventing back problems down the road. Many of them, especially the women, wear the cheapest tennis shoes they can find, making sure the better ones go to their children.

21

BBD&B

Baby Blankies, Books, Diapers and Birth Control

We have several people interested in providing birth control classes or individual discussions and are pretty much in agreement that having family planning discussions is a valuable and necessary topic to help families avoid "going under" financially, emotionally, psychologically and socially.

This is a complicated subject for many reasons—cultural, religious and personal. If we could help even a handful of people by giving them a safe place and sensitive, well-informed medical people to talk with, voice their needs and objections to birth control, fears, etc., I feel it would be worth it.

As of today, we have sources for handmade blankets, baby board books, diapers and a medical person willing to donate her time and training. Friends of Fieldworkers would pay for translators, as well. What we need is an accessible, safe venue to reach people who may be interested. As yet, we have none.

22

NEW BABY

When a family is expecting a new baby, we share the experience. I ask the mom if she needs prenatal vitamins and if she's going to the doctor and getting help with her diet.

As soon as she knows the baby's sex, we start collecting layette items, blankets, paper diapers, wipes and baby furnishings. We may get one or more of these items: bassinet, stroller, high chair, changing table, porta crib, car seat or swing. It really depends on what is requested, available or donated and what the family has room for.

Baby clothes are collected in these sizes: newborn, 0-3 months, 3-6 months, 6-9 months, 9 months, 12 months, and 18 months, maybe until 24 months or 2T. All baby clothes are washed in baby laundry soap, Dreft, and rinsed in white vinegar (Add 1/2 cup vinegar to the rinse cycle.) Christine Hodge, owner of the Ojai Apothecary, has provided baby bodywash and shampoo.

My personal favorite to give are baby board books. I collect these in English and Spanish, even Russian and French. Baby books, full of colorful pictures, need to be wiped clean with water and white vinegar. Magic Eraser sponges are the best for getting little smudges and black marks off the books. Babies cut their baby teeth on these and learn that books are a part of their lives from the earliest days. Some titles from naeyc.org are these:

Ten Little Fingers and Ten Little Toes by Mem Fox
Baby Bear, Baby Bear, What Do You See? by Bill Martin and Eric Carle
Global Babies from Global Fund for Children
I Am a Bunny and The Rooster Struts by Richard Scarry

Mommies Say Shhh! by Patricia Polacco
Bears by Ruth Krauss & Phyllis Rowand
!Pio Peep! Traditional Spanish Nursery Rhymes selected by Alma Flor Ada & F. Isabel Campoy
Families by Rena D. Grossman
Peekaboo Bedtime and Peekaboo Morning by Rachel Isadora
Hello, Day! by Anita Lobel
Mother Goose Picture Puzzles by Will Hillenbrand
My Farm Friends by Wendell Minor.

My personal favorites are any books by Todd Parr.

When delivering baby items, I usually bring along books and toys for the older siblings so they don't feel left out. Here are some good ideas for books about new babies from "The 10 Best Books For First Borns Who Are About To Become Big Brothers Or Sisters" By Elijah Brumback, September 02, 2016, on www.fatherly.com.

Ish by Peter H. Reynolds
Little Tadpole's Trouble by Tatyana Feeney
Benny & Beautiful Baby Delilah by Jean Van Leeuwen
O-L-I-V-E Marshmallow by Katie Saunders
Wolfie, The Bunny by Ame Dyckman
What Brothers Do Best by Laura Numeroff
Hello In There by Jo Witek
Little Miss, Big Sis by Amy Krouse Rosenthal and Peter H. Reynolds
Babies Don't Eat Pizza by Dianne Danzig
Ninja Baby by David Zeltser & Diane Goode.

http://sleepingshouldbeeasy.com
I'm A Big Brother or *I'm a Big Sister* by Joanna Cole
My New Baby by Rachel Fuller
We Have a Baby by Cathryn Falwell
The New Baby by Mercer Mayer
Everywhere Babies by Susan Meyers
The New Baby by Fred Rogers

23

FRUIT & STUFF STAND

I learned this from a young boy running his own fruit stand in Ojai, where he made regular change by putting out the fruit from the trees in his backyard. So that's how our Friends of Fieldworkers Fruit and Stuff Stand came to be. I made a sketch. Ted built it. We filled it with the oranges, lemons, tangerines, Mexican Limes and guavas from our trees. In addition, we discovered *Food Forward of Ventura County* which organizes volunteers to pick the excess fruit and vegetables from people's trees and gives them to local charities.

The local representative goes so far as to deliver the boxes of fruit to our door and to fill the fruit stand! I deliver most of the fresh fruit to fieldworkers' homes. Maybe a tenth of each delivery stays at the fruit stand for sale. And sometimes we give fresh fruit to those who support our work, as thank you's.

A hobby of mine is gardening. I have a little greenhouse created by the former owner of our home in Ojai, a Japanese gardener and plumber. I also have a special penchant for noticing succulents in town that need a bit of thinning. I can't blame the Master Gardener program I took upon moving into the Ojai Valley. But it did teach me the joy of propagation. My succulent arrangements find their way to the fruit stand and sell for $1-$10. Sometimes people leave their pots and plants there, too. My neighbor used to leave the excess eggs from her chickens.

Some weeks the money box (bolted and locked) has a few coins. Sometimes there are a few dollars. The biggest day was $21.52. ALL cash goes directly to fieldworkers—to children for the ice cream truck; for the mom needing diapers; for buying lunch at the zoo or for other incidentals involving our families.

Unfortunately, someone in our community didn't appreciate our sales project and reported us to the county which only *reacts to complaints*. We are country enough to have chickens and abundant fruit trees but not enough to have a fruit stand. My solution is to keep a jar of $5 bills on the refrigerator. Every day that I don't buy a coffee-shop coffee and treat, I transfer a bill into another jar. This will replace the fruit and stuff stand profit. This kills two birds with one stone, providing cash for a little FoF slush fund and curbing my afternoon sweets.

24

HEATERS & FANS

People living in tight, rundown quarters are often victims of fire. Our fieldworkers, especially those who have been in a fire, are afraid of their wall heaters. Rightly so. Landlords frequently fail to clean them or have the gas fixtures checked. I've seen these wall heaters covered by family photo collages, pictures of the Virgin Mary or pieces of brightly decorated cloth.

I've never been in a fieldworker's apartment in Oxnard or Port Hueneme that had air conditioning. And so, our families struggle with the cold and heat.

Two summers ago, I visited several families during a heatwave. Picture the family of 17 in a tiny space. Something had to be done. I called my friend, Jackie Treuting, a devout Catholic and social activist with her husband, John.

They are members of St. Jude the Apostle Catholic Church in Westlake Village whose slogan is *Jesus: Encountered. Loved. Served.* Their service group, Loaves and Fishes, hosts 15 ministries or outreaches in the community according to their website. They have helped our fieldworkers on more than one occasion.

I told Jackie about the heat. She had the request for fans put in their Sunday bulletin and within a week we had 13 fans, some new and still in their boxes. I picked them up from their garage and delivered them the next day. What a difference fans made!

Heaters are in equal demand during the winter. During the night, families can stay relatively warm under blankets sharing the heat of group-sleep. But especially in the early morning (4 or 5 a.m. when parents are preparing for work and getting the children ready for school or daycare), everyone suffers the cold. And so it is that all year round I purchase fans and heaters and store them in our garage for the next season's use. Do landlords complain about the higher electric bill? Sometimes, yes, they do.

25

DOUBLE JEOPARDY

Twice this year, one family has been struck with tragedy. Their two-year old daughter became susceptible to lung infections after heart surgery when she was a newborn. This January, she developed pneumonia and had to be helicoptered to a hospital in Los Angeles. Her Mixtec-speaking mother stayed home with her three older children who attend school. The toddler's father stayed in the hospital for two weeks around the clock with his little girl. While he was gone from home, we helped his wife and other children with food, water, diapers, books, toys and encouragement. When the toddler was well enough to come home, Ted and I drove down to Los Angeles and brought them back to Oxnard. While she slept, her dad was able to unwind and tell us all about their hospital experience.

In July, the same family sent their two eldest children to Mexico to meet their grandparents for the very first time. They talked so lovingly of their family and the time they had together—walking in the mountains, seeing new animals, trees, flowers they'd never seen before and being fed and pampered by their grandparents.

Unfortunately, however, the children returned after a few weeks covered in mosquito bites. GA's leg and ankle were terribly infected after riding a bus for two days and not having clean water for washing her bites. The parents immediately took GA to the doctor who treated her with antibiotics; they were not effective. After rigorous treatment, the doctor was afraid that she might have some flesh-eating infection and had her rushed by helicopter to another hospital.

Again, this devoted father stayed with his daughter (10 years old) where the doctors warned him they might have to amputate her leg or she could possibly die if they couldn't get the infection under control. You can imagine how her worried mother was feeling at home, unable to even visit her daughter in the hospital. The doctors were afraid to expose the other children to this unknown disease.

I visited RA and GA soon after she was admitted, and he and I shared a meal in the hospital kitchen. We purchased a meal card so he could eat something other than what came off the meal trays brought to his daughter's room.

While father and daughter were in the hospital, we spoke nearly every day to get updates on her status and on his family at home. We took some meals, groceries, diapers, toys, and hot meals to them. We helped pay their utilities with the support of All Saints Episcopal Church in Oxnard.

When GA felt better, we mailed books, puzzles, coloring books, paints, colored pencils and Barbie dolls with clothes—her favorite. She couldn't get out of bed much and was very bored much of the time when not sleeping. Reading books out loud to her dad provided some comfort.

During one of her surgeries to remove the infection, her dad and I waited together in the surgery waiting room. It was very frightening because the doctors were not sure what the outcome would be. Thank God and all the people who were praying for her, the news was good. No amputation.

When we picked them up three weeks later and delivered them to their home, GA and RA were thrilled to see their family again and to eat familiar food. GA was fitted with an amazing medical advancement, a machine which removed the "bad blood" into a little bag attached to her leg and circulated "good blood" to the spot on her ankle that had opened up to a ragged six or seven-inch wound. After being home for about four months, GA's incision closed up completely, much to the doctors' amazement. Her other vertical incision also healed well. It is a miracle, they say. But a very long ordeal for the family. Thankfully, after a few months of healing and with a teacher coming to her home, GA is back in her classroom healthy and doing well with her studies.

26

CRISIS REFERRALS

We get referrals from churches and the Ventura County Pediatric Diagnostic Center where families bring their sick babies and children for treatment or surgery. We have provided food, clothing, toys, bedding, diapers, books, toys, and utility payments as needed, in addition to moral support.

For children taking chemotherapy or recovering from surgery resulting in weakened immune systems, we provide bleach, Lysol disinfectant wipes and disinfectant hand soaps and wipes.

Whether the children need two to four surgeries for a cleft palate or three years of treatment for cancer, we are there to supply our support, including basic needs. Plus, the other siblings in the home need some special attention, too. It's very rewarding work.

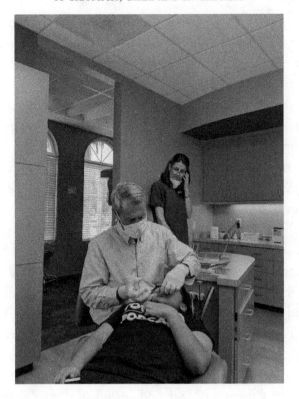

27

SMILE POWER

If eyes are the window of the soul, smiles are the doors. Dental braces made a big difference for my three children, myself and other members of my family. They were confidence-builders and frankly, in modern times, they are a bit of a status symbol. Also, one's teeth reveal self-care and personal pride. In the long term, healthy and aligned teeth do affect overall health.

A few years ago, when we first met LH, a lovely thirteen-year-old girl, I was moved by the light and fire in her eyes and the contrasting restraint in her smile. My granddaughter Maddy was the same age and starting her second round of orthodontia an hour away in Santa Monica. She and her mother Jennie, my daughter, decided LH should have the same opportunity, so Jennie contributed $500 through Friends of Fieldworkers so we could make the down payment for the orthodontist.

For the next 18 months or so, we trekked down to Santa Monica to see her dentist and make it a special outing. We shopped or ate at new restaurants or played on the beach. If sore teeth prevented a regular meal, we stopped at KFC for mashed potatoes. Fro-Yo was another favorite.

Sometimes her two brothers joined us, and LH and I chatted like magpies during the drive with them in the back seat, listening to music on headphones. On alone trips, we had a great time talking about anything, everything or nothing. Undivided attention.

We both had mixed emotions when the braces came off. Happy for her beautiful smile; sad for the end of ortho trips.

When we met our next young woman who required braces, we treaded lightly. Would we insult her by mentioning the need? As it turns out, she and her parents had already considered the possibility and the high cost. They were delighted that Friends of Fieldworkers would be willing to help her.

We located an orthodontist through friends. I sent a letter of request to Dr. Christoph Haar and included a letter from our teen explaining why braces were important to her overall life plan. We made an appointment and it was a match made in heaven. We discovered that some extractions were required, and he even asked another dentist friend, Dr. Greg Wolfe, to help out. Their fees were greatly reduced and spaced over several months. We did GoFundMe campaigns for Ted's and my birthdays which helped pay the dentists. We will forever be grateful to these two highly-skilled, kind and generous men and to their staffs for their care of SN.

28

MEAL SHARES

On more than one occasion a family has invited me to stay and eat with them when I visited their home. Since I live in Ojai, about thirty-five minutes from our nearest family, I try to see three or four families each time I go visiting. I also go in the late afternoon or early evening to make sure I catch the families at home from school and work. This means I frequently drop in around dinner time.

I might be delivering clothes, books or school supplies or talking with the children about how they were doing in school. One of the mothers in the family would be cooking tortillas on their apartment stove or stirring soup. They would ask me to sit down at the table and bring me a plate.

One such meal particularly sticks in my mind. I was given a brown-colored soup with bits of spicy meat in it and some type of vegetables. Tortillas right off the griddle smelled delicious. I asked for a spoon for the soup. When they brought it to me, I was the only one using one. The other diners scooped up the soup with the tortillas.

I remember feeling very happy and accepted as one of the family. It reminded me of eating in the home of a classmate in Hawaii where I grew up or in the home of an Acoma Indian on the reservation in New Mexico where I taught first and second grade. I felt right at home.

Strawberry Woman by Roxie Ray, www.RoxieRay.com

29

CHECK-INS

In the month following the two big fires mentioned earlier, I contacted the families frequently. *How are you? Is everyone well? Are you working? How are you doing for rent? for food? for school supplies? clothes? What do you need now?*

Of course, after the disasters, there were lots of needs because families were practically starting from scratch. However, as the months and years go by, I check in less frequently. Usually their needs decrease or at least change as things get back to normal for them.

If a family has another kind of trouble like a sick or injured child, I call them much more frequently; daily, if they are in a hospital. I consider myself their extended family since most of them have no or few relatives living here. When bad things happen, there's no one or few to call. Sometimes a Mixtec and Spanish-speaking mom who knows I don't speak either language, will text me a photo of her child in a hospital bed. Then I know to have someone call her back. Once, a young mother I knew very well called and spoke to me in Spanish. Later, her husband told me that she was so frightened and just wanted to hear my voice. What a gift that was to me. Meaningful and touching.

When things are going smoothly for a family, I usually back off and call or stop by every few months or so.

Because I speak so little Spanish, there are some real hazards. And, as anyone who works with families of a different language knows, it can be dangerous, or at least confusing, to rely on the children as translators. I'm embarrassed to say that I have asked children as young as kindergarteners to explain what their parent was telling me. Thankfully, apart from the hospital NICU fiasco, mentioned later, I usually get by without disastrous effects. I have even been known to stop someone in Target or on the street to talk to a farmworker on the phone to interpret. Or I call AR, RA, JA or PV to help me. It's not ideal but it works pretty well.

LEVEL 2

SAFETY: HOUSING, SECURITY, STABILITY & LAW

30
HOUSING INSECURITY

When a family of five lost their 29-year-old father/provider to a sudden heart attack this winter, they had no means of support. FoF was out of funds at the time. Thankfully, another beautiful example of serendipity occurred as it so often does. Tiffany Lewis called me from the Democratic Club of Camarillo, asking if she could learn about Friends of Fieldworkers. I told her about this family's loss. She called the head of the Democratic Mom's Club, Martha Martinez-Bravo. Between the two of them and their connections, they raised money for the family's rent, food, clothing, food, diapers and toys. This gave the family some time to plan what to do after the funeral. We were able to take some home-cooked meals, boxes of fruit and vegetables (from The Abundant Table in Camarillo) and to get a beautiful hand-made quilt for each of the five members of the family from Darla Drain in Port Hueneme, and her Outlaw Quilters' Club.

Fortunately, the family was able to move into a smaller, more affordable place and the mother was able to find work in a restaurant. What we did was to provide a security net and buy them some time. Farmworkers can sometimes depend on their families for help during the hard times. But when there is a severe injury, illness, death, fire or flood, families really suffer. They feel alone and isolated.

31

SECTION 8 PRIVILEGE

One couple signed up for Section 8 Housing when their first child was born. They were living in someone's garage "apartment" (10 ft. X 10 ft) with a closet-sized bathroom, portable sink, refrigerator and queen-sized mattress on the floor. They had a child's table and chair for their daughter. After waiting for seven years, they got a letter of approval for Section 8 Housing.

It gave them a brief time limit to find a property that would accept Section 8. Unfortunately, in Ventura County, there are very few available apartments that do.

Together, PV and I contacted about twenty apartment complex managers. No luck. Finally, when she applied to an apartment near her daughter's school, she was told there was a six to twelve month waiting list. We later talked with the manager who repeated what her secretary had said. I left my Friends of Fieldworkers business card and expressed my dismay at this unfair, unforgiving system.

The following day the manager called to tell PV that they had an opening but couldn't show the apartment until the day of the move-in. Whoever heard of that? Sight-unseen rental! And this Title 8 privilege dropped her rent only $100/month. It costs the couple $1128 for a one-bedroom apartment!

32

MOVE-INS

Whether a family is moving into a garage, a single bedroom of another's house, or their own apartment, they often start with nothing.

Here is a general list that I like to go by in finding items for a move-in. Of course, there are some items more critical than others.

1) mattress, twin, double or queen-sized, depending on how many sleepers there will be. Generally, 2-6 share one mattress on the floor. St. Vincent de Paul and Goodwill sometimes provide vouchers for these.
2) pillows, blankets and sometimes sheets (not always used)
3) plastic hangers and laundry baskets
4) narrow chest of drawers 4-6 ft. tall

5) trashcan for bedroom and bathroom

6) towels, washrags and bath mats

7) toilet brush, sponges

8) shower curtain and rings (if not provided)

9) sofa or sofa-bed

10) bookcase

11) small table (no sharp corners)

12) 1-2 table lamps or standing lamp with bulbs

13) for babies if parents want them:

    small apartment-sized crib

    highchair

    changing table with storage

    diaper pail or genie with bags

    musical swing

    walker with toys

14) welcome mat

15) paper items (paper towels, napkins, toilet paper, Kleenex)

16) kitchen or dining room table and chairs (compact ones are best)

17) medium microwave

18) blender

19) dishes & bowls, serving bowls

20) silverware

21) kitchen towels and washrags

22) plastic or glass storage containers with lids

23) pitcher

24) toaster or toaster oven

25) dish pan and rack

26) mixing spoons & bowls

27) cooking tools (spatulas, slotted spoons)

28) cutting board (also used for making tortillas)

29) knives

30) quilts (one for each member of the family, if possible)

31) garbage can for kitchen & bags

32) faucet filter for kitchen sink (to avoid buying water in bottles)

33) corn broom, dustpan, mop and bucket

34) frying pan (large)

35) large cook pot with lid

36) 3-4 pots with lids (varying sizes)

I also provide rice pots, crock pots, electric juicers and most recently, water filters, if they are interested in using them. It will save them a lot of money. And if I know the family very well, I even provide paintings for the wall, cannister sets, calendars, crosses and other homey things. See section, "Grocery List" for other useful items to have at move-in.

33

WELCOME MAT

Fieldworkers are mostly immigrants from somewhere else and are not unfortunately, made to feel welcome in our country. Which is so bizarre to me because we depend on them to do so many jobs that we won't do or are unable to do.

Sometimes I go up to strangers who speak in a different language or with a strong accent and ask them where they are from and just say, *Welcome to America. We are glad you are here.* My grown children have warned me that asking strangers, cab drivers and others on the street where they are from is not really cool, kosher or politically correct. But I feel most people understand where I'm coming from and forgive the intrusion. Being a white-haired elder has its advantages. People figure I am just old and don't know better.

Sometimes I just like to give fieldworkers a visual reminder that they are welcome...at least in their own home. I look for sales or use coupons to buy welcome mats. Decent ones are $20-$25 and I simply drop them off at their door. A little welcome treat. *Welcome Home. Glad to See You. Hooray, you're Home. You're Back!* That sort of thing.

34

PAPER GOODS

Toilet paper, paper towels, feminine pads, and Kleenex. It is simple to buy an extra of each item when we shop and store the items in a box in the hall closet. Then we distribute to families on our visits. Because of the cost of housing in our area, people often rent one room of an apartment or the garage of a house (think dark, airless and shared with auto parts, gas and oil cans). There's usually one bathroom for up to 17 members of a household. As I mentioned before, because toilet paper is expensive and not reusable, each family group keeps their own toilet paper in their own room and carries it back and forth to the bathroom. I don't remember ever seeing a box of Kleenex in homes, so I guess that's sometimes why the runny noses. One's necessity is another's luxury.

35

GARAGE LIVING

Until we began working with farmworkers in Ventura County, I'd never heard of anyone living in a garage and sharing space with car parts, cans of gas and oil, lawnmowers, old clothes and stored items spilling over from the house. There is limited light and ventilation. There may be roaches, rats, ants, spiders and other creatures. Think about your own garage. Could you comfortably sleep, eat, dress, talk on your phone, visit with your children and help them with their homework in there? With maybe one overhead light or just a table lamp?

From Coast and Valley Property Management newsletter we read:

Individual municipalities may have even more specific laws. Garages in California need to meet these basic requirements to count as a habitable space.

- *Natural ventilation that is at least 1/20 the size of the floor space or 5 square feet at a minimum.*
- *Sleeping areas need a window that is no more than 44 inches off the ground. Also, has an opening of at least 5.7 square feet.*
- *Ceilings need to be at least 7 feet and 6 inches in height.*
- *Heating that keeps rooms at a temperature at 70 degrees for at least 3 feet above the floor.*
- *Rooms must have natural light that is at least 10 percent the size of the square footage.*
- *A room used for sleeping cannot have a garage open into the room.*
- *All rooms need a smoke detection device installed.*
- *The room requires at least one wall controlled light switch.*
- *Electrical wall outlets need spacing to ensure that no part of the floor is more than 6 feet away from an outlet.*
- *The room cannot have a gas water heater in it if it is a sleeping space.*

In addition to meeting all the state and city codes for building, safety, and housing standards, landlords must ensure that any unit they rent out has:

- *Heating*
- *Hot and cold water with working plumbing*
- *Electricity*
- *No pests or mold*
- *Intact doors, windows, and roofs that resist weather*
- *A sewage disposal system*
- *Standard safety features like locks*
- *A lack of obvious hazards*

https://www.coastandvalleypm.com/is-it-illegal-to-live-in-a-garage-in-california/

No, I don't think people in garages complain if their living arrangement is not up to code. It would be too dangerous for them to do so.

I once asked one of our families that had survived the 2013 Oxnard Fire to allow a mother and her 3-year-old daughter seeking asylum from Mexico to rent a bedroom from them. They said she could live in their garage until a bedroom was vacated by the present renters, a family of 4. For the privilege, this mother was charged $400/month which Friends of Fieldworkers paid for her. We also provided a portable heater and fan, twin beds, a dresser, book shelf, two lamps, laundry baskets, bath and bed linens in addition to clothing, food gift cards, and transportation to her doctors' and Immigration appointments. One of our other families we'd helped in the past, took them under their wings, befriending and helping them in a variety of ways, including a trip to the emergency room.

Although this rental was better than being on the street, it really troubled me to visit this family of two. Cars belong in a garage, not people. Unfortunately, this happens very frequently in our county.

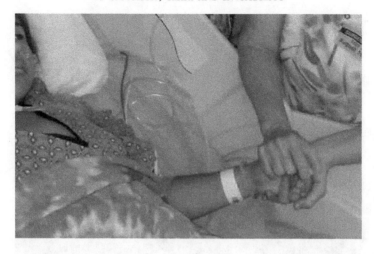

36

HOSPITAL VISITS

I visit children in the hospital when they are sick or injured. I visited one young boy with cystic fibrosis in a local hospital and a young girl in another hospital an hour away who had badly infected mosquito bites. We also provided transportation home from a Los Angeles hospital to a toddler child, recovering from pneumonia. It helps to take an assortment of coloring books, helium balloons (if allowed by the hospital), crayons, colored pencils or pens, books, puzzles, and favorite snacks (if allowed) such as fresh fruit or Takis Fuego Hot Chili Pepper & Lime Tortilla chips or apple juice boxes. Little cars and dolls are also popular with kids sick in bed. Stuffed animals and soft blankets are good for little ones. Once I was able to relieve mom and dad for a few minutes and the young patient taught me how to do Snapchat on my iPhone and his iPad.

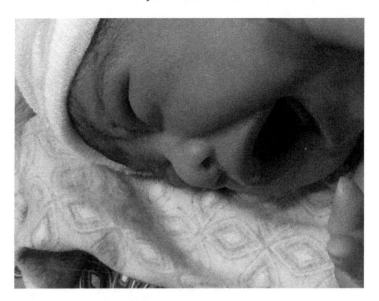

37

BIRTH PARTNER

I'd known this young woman for about five years since she was referred to us. There were many reasons for me to admire and appreciate her, but one was how she handled challenges in her life—even things she wanted, such as another child. It was eight years since her first child was born and her own mom lives behind the WALL and isn't available to help.

Birthing is a vulnerable time where you really need your partner or mother or someone very close to you present. Usually there is a grandmother or sister or other female friend who can share the labor experience. My friend's mother lives as far away as the moon, for all practical purposes. I knew this and so I offered to be with her during her son's birth. She never replied so I forgot about it.

One day while I was preparing lunch, I got this text:

She: I'm in the hospital. Baby coming.
Me: Where?
She: St. John's

I called the labor and delivery department and told them I'd be there as quickly as I could, about a (fast) 25-minute drive from Ojai. When I got there, the nurse took me right in to the birthing suite and told her, *She's here now.*

We had an intimate and memorable time together; she talked about God and her family between contractions. I held her hand and told her how brave she was and what a great job she was doing. She made no sound during contractions. Her healthy baby boy was born sixty minutes later and the doctor asked if I'd like to cut his cord. What a moment it was! His father, aunt and uncle arrived immediately after, from work, and I went home, feeling blessed.

38

HONORABLE APPOINTMENTS

I am privileged to take our friends to their appointments and make sure there are translators in Mixtec or at least in Spanish. When the young father's eye was injured in a basketball game, he went to several doctors before his surgery. I met him and his wife, and two young daughters at one ophthalmologist's office and sat in on his appointment. I also made some calls on his behalf to the surgeon's office and hospital to discuss payment options. Friends of Fieldworkers helped with some of those bills which were thankfully reduced. Yes, employers provide workers with insurance but usually only for those accidents that occur on the job. Additional insurance is available but often just too expensive.

I drove one young mother and her teenager to a legal appointment in Los Angeles. I've taken two teens to their dental and orthodontic appointments. I've spoken with the Housing Authority, Police Department, Immigration attorneys, I.C.E. police, real estate agents, apartment managers, and nurse practitioners. I've also written letters on our fieldworker friends' behalf as an advocate from Friends of Fieldworkers, Inc. Sometimes I didn't open my mouth except to introduce myself and hand over my business card. The support was in just being there.

39
MISTAKEN IDENTITY

A family called to say that one of their members had gotten a very disturbing letter from a government agency in the county. It stated that he owed a large amount of money and was being sued in small claims court. He was requested to respond within 14 days or have serious consequences. The parents were distraught. The children were upset. Any unexpected request for money (which they do not have) leads to thoughts of jail and deportation.

I stopped in to see the letter and got the person's permission, in writing, to call the company on his behalf. As it turns out, there are many people in Ventura County with the same first and last name. After I got past the first person to the supervisor, I was told that this letter was indeed, meant for another person by the same name at a different address. Mistaken identity. I can only imagine how many times this has happened. People's lives have been interrupted and they've been unduly frightened by someone else's mistake.

40
I.C.E. AGE

Last year our area of Southern California experienced one of the worst fires in California history and then floods and mud flows in neighboring Montecito that killed several people, including my sister's brother-in-law. Our quaint little town of Ojai had months of fire-smoke-recovery and it was pretty awful. People were still in shock over the near destruction of Ojai. And then one day with burnt-out trees, homes and hillsides all around us, there were I.C.E. officers in unmarked cars in our neighborhood streets. They were there in the morning when parents were taking their children to school and as they were driving to work. I.C.E. waited there after school and

after work. They waited at stop signs looking for, what they admitted to other city officers, "people of color driving older cars." This is deplorable. According to one website, California is home to 39% people of color.
http://worldpopulationreview.com/states/california-population/

I.C.E. (Immigration and Custom Enforcement) even stopped a mom at the McDonald's a mile from my house in Mira Monte where she was getting her son a hamburger before his ball game. No one was safe. Anywhere, it seemed.

When I got wind of this from a friend, I felt I needed to do something. I went to the offices of our Police and Sheriff Departments, to the local newspaper, and the office of our mayor. I wrote a letter to our local representative. Here is one of the follow-up letters I wrote.

February 16, 2018
Sergeant Peter C. Seery
Ventura County Police Department

Dear Sergeant Seery,

Thank you for returning to the office to talk with me in your office yesterday. We were questioning I.C.E. reportedly conducting Ojai Valley operations. Today these exact words are on the *Ojai Valley News* front page.

Fire, floods and I.C.E.– hard to say which is most destructive. In our valley, "A City of Peace" the first two may not be preventable. I empathized with your and Captain Slominski's positions that the rules of this department of the federal government have changed. I had an appointment with Mayor Johnston today, as well. You all may be as caught off-guard and horrified as we are.

You warned me that tackling an unmarked, suspicious vehicle is dangerous. You stated that I should always call your department immediately for you to investigate suspicious situations, taking photos, only if feasible.

Yesterday I had a yard sale and set up a fruit stand "Stand for Farmworkers" at my home. Two sheriff cars drove by and I wondered if I were being watched. I can imagine how immigrants feel (regardless of their status) when they take their kids to school, drive to work or go to buy diapers at Rite Aid.

Just a clarification. *Illegal Alien* has been replaced with *Undocumented* or *Unauthorized Immigrants*. In 1970 *Illegal Alien* replaced *Wetback*. Americans and English evolve...slowly.

http://thehill.com/blogs/pundits-blog/immigration/331586-alienated-its-time-to-abandon-the-term-illegal-alien

Working for peace and justice for all,
Judy Fisk Lucas

41

COURTHOUSE

I once went with a middle-aged man to his court date. He spoke Mixtec and a little Spanish, so I was there mainly as moral support at the request of a mutual friend and to make sure he had a Mixtec interpreter assigned to his case. He was charged with a DUI and I probably wouldn't have gone if it hadn't been for the special request from my friend, and the fact that he and his wife lived in a garage with their four children, one of whom was severely disabled. The child was not expected to live past his first birthday but had made it by then, to his 8th and now, to his 11th. He could not do anything for himself and I was amazed by the bravery and loving care his parents gave him around the clock. Frankly, I couldn't imagine his mother doing all this alone.

I went into chambers with him, his Anglo court-appointed attorney and the Spanish translator, not a Mixteco one. Spanish was his second language so I wondered how much was lost in translation.

People in most cultures drink alcohol and take drugs to dull the pain, among other things. That's one reason. If there is a proclivity for alcoholism and a set of circumstances that seem impossible to overcome and a feeling of hopelessness, drinking becomes a vicious cycle.

The judge said that this wasn't his first offence and he should probably give him jail time but then he'd be deported for sure. He gave him the option of a residential alcohol program where he'd have to stay for a few months.

I called several times to follow-up with the program director to see if my friend needed anything and how he was doing. I got one call returned over the time he was in "treatment." I learned that he was allowed to go to work during the day to support his family. And then he was allowed to spend the night at home to help his family. I didn't really understand this rehabilitation process. And at the end of the program, he and his family returned to their family in Mexico.

Now, three years later, his wife and children are back in California again, without their dad, and she supports them by working in the fields. Our mutual friend found a sponsor for the family and they are allowed to stay because of the child, now a teenager, and his special needs. They are in their own apartment living near a family member in the same complex. I never cease being inspired by the determination and resourcefulness of our families. Nothing stops them from fighting for their children.

Friends of Fieldworkers provided some furniture, bedding and bath linens, clothing, diapers and other paper goods, kitchen and bath supplies and a full pantry and freezer. Backpacks, school supplies, toys, books and their own bookcase, of course. I advocated for a wheelchair and special school placement for this disabled teenager which he got within a week or two. Others had been working on this for a very long time and maybe it was just the normal wait-time. However, I've noticed that being the president of a nonprofit charity and an advocate for fieldworkers does open a few doors. But not all doors, and some, very slowly.

Since it was Christmas, we also brought a tree, lights and decorations, and an invitation from Camarillo ACTION's Christmas Shoppe so they'd have wrapped presents under the tree. And because their family lived next door and had children of the same ages, we duplicated many of the same things for them, too. The final touch was the Welcome Home mat. They deserve this and so much more.

42

HOTLINE/GRAPEVINE

Celery Harvest by Roxie Ray, www.RoxieRay.com

News of I.C.E. activity in a neighborhood or speculations about work shortages, pesticide sprayings and other injustices spread quickly through fieldworker communities. But when a family encounters their own shortage of food, clothing, diapers, rent money and medical help, they often remain isolated in their pain. Many cycles of seasonal work have taught them to save for times of work slowdown. Savings often go under the mattress (literally) because of the impracticality and costs of banking. And fear.

This works well unless there's a fire or an injury on-the-job preventing workers from doing their job. I learned from one of my friends that because they work with fresh fruit and vegetables, their bodies are regularly checked for cuts or other imperfections. Wearing a bandage warrants being sent home. Without pay. And yet, their work around machinery, tools, heavy boxes, irregular terrain, and thorny fruit vines makes safety a constant concern.

For these reasons, we have considered creating a hotline specifically for fieldworkers to call about sensitive issues of deportation, legalization, work complaints, paycheck injustices, medical needs, housing, etc. Here is another chance to team-up with an existing resource such as 2-1-1 in Ventura County, the easy-to-remember three-digit telephone number to dial for information and referrals to health, human and social service organizations.

From their website:

2-1-1, a program of <u>Interface Children & Family Services</u>, is the comprehensive information and referral service for Ventura County. We connect over 30,000 Ventura County callers and texters each year with information about health and human services available to them.

2-1-1 Ventura County phone and text services are available 24 hours a day, 7 days a week. 2-1-1 is available in 150 languages through phone interpretation services.

Launched on February 11, 2005, 2-1-1 Ventura County was the first live 2-1-1 in the state of California. Interface added texting to 2-1-1 "call or click" services in February 2017, becoming one of few 2-1-1's nationwide to offer two-way texting available 24/7 in English and Spanish. 2-1-1 Ventura County also provides resources to over 3,000 unique visitors each month through the <u>211Ventura.org</u> website.

When one of our moms requested a source for diapers and childcare in the community, I suggested we dial 2-1-1 together. We were pleasantly surprised when they were able to get a Mixtec-speaker on the line within five minutes who had some practical suggestions to offer. There's room to expand this service. I did go to the Interface Children & Family

Services office to get some 2-1-1 cards and flyers and passed them out to our families. The office manager said many undocumented farmworkers are afraid to use this service because of their ever-present fear of detection. And even flyers written in Spanish aren't very effective since not all fieldworkers read in their second language.

43

PROFESSIONAL POOL

Dr. Robert Jordan, a dermatologist in Ventura, treated one woman's facial burn scars for free. Dr. Christoph Haar and Dr. Greg Wolfe, in Ojai and Ventura, treated another teen, and provided her with braces at one third the normal cost. Vanessa Frank, immigration attorney, has seen two or three of our fieldworkers, very reasonably, untangling their complicated legal issues.

I envision a pool of medical, dental, educational, legal and other professionals who can be consulted when fieldworkers have specific needs. It's been suggested that the best way to build such a team is to visit service groups such as Rotary, Lions and Soroptimist Clubs to share these stories and to ask for help.

44

KEEPING IN TOUCH

During the Thomas Fire of 2017, Ted and I left our home in Ojai because of the fire, the smoke and unhealthy air quality. We were gone for a month, staying in our motorhome in different parks and in a friend's driveway in Camarillo over the Christmas holidays. Several of our fieldworker friends called us over the month to see if we were alright. One of our fieldworker friends called us nearly every day that month, just to check in, even while her own husband was still working in the smoky fields inadequately protected.

I called many of our farmworkers throughout the county and was horrified to hear that many of them were still working in the fields in spite of unsafe, smoky conditions. It was hard for them to breathe. They had no choice but to continue working. We did contribute some face masks to one group who delivered them to workers in the fields. It was a very disturbing sight to see workers struggling to harvest the crops in those inhumane conditions.

In the months to come, workers were treated for various fire and smoke-related illnesses. They have few if any safety nets even in these extreme weather conditions. This is true of all kinds of weather—rain, wind, dust storms, freezing cold and blazing heat.

I feel helpless in these situations. I can call and check on them. I can take heaters or fans or masks or sun hats. But I can't make it any easier for them in the fields.

45

SAFETY NETS

This is a continuation of the last story. Two brothers, their wives and six children between them, moved into a two-bedroom apartment after the 2013 fire. All four parents work in the fields. The wives only took time off for having a baby or an extended illness. Both families are very active in two different churches and spend Sundays having family outings at the beach, park or in the mountains. Occasionally, one of the fathers plays pick-up basketball with his friends. In one such game, he was elbowed in the eye, breaking a bone and blood vessels.

For a month or so he hoped and prayed that his double vision would improve with rest. Eventually, after being seen by two or three doctors, it was decided that he required surgery. I went with him, his wife and daughters to one of his pre-surgery appointments.

Although the hospital bill would be $12,000 for a patient with regular medical insurance, his own medical insurance didn't cover it because the injury was not work-related. They were able to set him up with an account and discount the bill, allowing him to pay monthly, on a sliding scale.

His surgeon also discounted his bill to $1600, but insisted on being paid that amount on the day before surgery. To this day I don't know how they scraped together $1,000 but he was still short. Then we put the balance on our family credit card which he could pay off by doing yard work, which he did. He was unable to go back to work in the fields for about three months. He did get minimal disability pay but it had a big impact on the family's income. Today he's back in the fields with minor limitations to his vision. In order for the double vision and eye pain when he lifts heavy loads to completely go away, he'd require more surgery. He says that he'll live with it.

46

COMPASSIONATE BANKS

Muhammad Yunus wrote *Banker to The Poor: Micro-Lending and the Battle Against World Poverty*, with Alan Jolis, in New York, 2007. This was after he founded the Grameen Bank in Bangladesh in 1976 for which he won a Nobel Prize. This inspiring, passionate man spoke at CSU Channel Islands a few years ago. The whole idea of microfinance fascinated me. After working with fieldworkers and seeing how much of their hard-earned money goes into the pockets of payday check cashers and money-lenders, I think this would be revolutionary.

The following comes from https://www.paydayloaninfo.org/facts

Payday loans in the United States range in size from $100 to $1,000, depending on state legal maximums. The average loan term is about two weeks. Loans typically cost 400% annual interest (APR) or more. The finance charge ranges from $15 to $30 to borrow $100.

The Federal Trade Commission Consumer Information site
describes payday loans: https://www.consumer.ftc.gov

*A payday loan — that is, a cash advance secured by a personal check or
paid by electronic transfer is very expensive credit. How expensive? Say you
need to borrow $100 for two weeks. You write a personal check for $115, with
$15 the fee to borrow the money. The check casher or payday lender agrees to
hold your check until your next payday. When that day comes around, either
the lender deposits the check and you redeem it by paying the $115 in cash,
or you roll-over the loan and are charged $15 more to extend the financing
for 14 more days. If you agree to electronic payments instead of a check, here's
what would happen on your next payday: the company would debit the full
amount of the loan from your checking account electronically or extend the
loan for an additional $15. The cost of the initial $100 loan is a $15 finance
charge and an annual percentage rate of 391 percent. If you roll-over the
loan three times, the finance charge would climb to $60 to borrow the $100.*

*Summary: money costs the most for people who need it most and have
the least. This is injustice at its worst. We need bankers with imagination
and compassion to start a great social business right here, right now.*

47

LIBRARY MISUNDERSTANDINGS

I like to take our children on "fieldtrips" to their nearest library. We
pick up the forms, partially fill them out and explain that they need a
parent's signature for permission to borrow books. Some parents may
resist because in small living quarters with many people, items can get
lost or ruined. I understand that. It's like getting a new puppy. There
needs to be some prior understandings...

One little boy I took refused to even enter the library. I discovered
that he'd lost his books in the Oxnard house fire. He was convinced
that the local library police were looking for him and probably going
to deport him. Well, that myth was busted.

I took him to the head librarian and we shared his story. Fortunately, she was very understanding and could help. After giving him an explanation of how libraries work, she wiped his record clean and gave him a new card. When we got to his home, we talked with his family about having a special place for his library books and card.

For any child, but particularly ones with limited resources and personal belongings, a library card can be magical. I encourage the children to choose books about their interests at different levels. Even if they can't read all of them, it gives them a vision of scope on a topic. And it's empowering, even if they can only read the lowest level books.

48

REGISTRATION, LICENSE & AUTO INSURANCE

One young man was referred to us because of some unusual hardships he'd suffered. The first thing on the agenda was to help him become a legal driver. He had a reliable car he was driving but without a current license, registration or auto insurance. In order to drive to work, he needed to satisfy those requirements.

A supporter-friend and I took him to Julio's Insurance Agency in Oxnard to get auto insurance, to the DMV to get his registration and then to Ventura County Office Building in Ventura to address his unpaid tickets, which we learned of in the process. The office was very helpful in giving him extra time with reduced payments so that he could meet his obligations. Keeping everything current and paid up-to-date was now up to him.

49

SCHOOL ADVOCATE

A child with special needs was having trouble in school so I asked the parents' permission to get involved with the school district. I requested a school psychologist, special testing and another appropriate program placement if necessary. I pursued this for one young teen who had severe educational, emotional and social issues and after several visits with the family, the school and the school psychologist, a true miracle happened. He was offered placement in a non-public special education school at the district's expense. Almost unheard of.

Unfortunately, the placement did not work out because the student refused to attend. I never was able to find out the real reason why. As a friend used to say, *Sometimes you eat the bear and sometimes the bear eats you.* This was an incredibly big disappointment.

Fortunately, we have had other more successful opportunities to advocate for children in school when we arrange to talk with our children's teachers about their achievement in school and how they can improve with some support. We need some retired teachers who love kids and have experience with ESL (English as a Second Language) students.

50

CAR SEATS

One family lost all three of their car seats in the Oxnard fire of 2013 and asked if we could help them. I contacted the Pregnancy Center in Ventura which has the *Earn While You Learn program*; the Ventura County Public Health *Safe Kids Program;* V.C. Medical Center's *Injury Prevention Program* and finally, the Ventura County Fire Department Regional Training Facility in Camarillo, which provided the family with three car seats, instructions and help with installation.

This brought to my attention the bind that families are in when they have to, by law and common sense, protect their children while riding in a vehicle. But car seats are expensive and harder and harder to find second-hand because of their expiration dates. Most thrift stores no longer sell them. Hospitals do not provide them. Another double bind for fieldworkers. One nonprofit, however, is a good place to start.

From the Reference.com site:

https://www.reference.com/vehicles/wic-car-seat-program-d2b4e 3252844f916

WIC (Women, Infants and Children) offices should be the first places checked when in desperate need of a car seat. For those already enrolled in the WIC program, ask WIC about their free car seat program. To obtain the seat, a class is required to be taken. The class can be from one hour to about two hours long. Car seat safety is taught as is how to properly install a seat. Once the class is completed, a voucher is given for a free car seat.

51

BLANKIES & BOOKS

Most fieldworkers' children do not own their own books since family funds are needed for basics: food, water, rent, utilities and gas for their cars so they can get to work. Children introduced early to books and reading have a much better success rate in school and a broader picture of the world. If we want all children to succeed, we must provide them with their own books.

I figured that pairing books with blankets was a good move. Two comfort measures together. Maybe even three. Reading books, wrapped in a blanket on a parent or sibling's lap are a great combination. How to get these to children?

The organization *First Five* or *Neighborhood for Learning* serves children ages 0-5. I delivered hundreds of board books, picture books and baby blankets to chapters of these organizations in Ojai, El Rio, Port Hueneme and Oxnard. They then distributed them to moms and babies in their education classes. Last week Camarillo's Mount Cross Lutheran Church Preschool delivered seven boxes of like-new books they collected over the past few months to one of our First Five locations.

And fortunately, another hobby of mine is collecting children's books. When I attended graduate school at the University of New Mexico, my children were 18 months, 2 1/2 and 4 1/2. They attended the university childcare co-op and some of our best memories involved the children's section of the university library. I took a Children's Literature course which opened new doors for me and my children. Nearly twenty years later I helped to get the Children's Library created at CSU Channel Islands which reaches hundreds of children (maybe thousands) in Ventura County.

To all our fieldworker families we offer libraries-in-a-box. As simple as a plastic milk crate or as fancy as an oak bookcase, these contain an assortment of children's books. And I always keep children's books in the FoF van when visiting families. It's not unusual for children in the neighborhood to run to the FoF van asking for books!

Here is a site for educators and families of English language learners which provides an annotated list of board books and more in Spanish: Hispanic Heritage.

¡Coloring Colorado!: http://www.colorincolorado.org/booklist/board-books-and-more-hispanic-heritage

Thrift stores, yard sales, and the Friends of the Library used bookstores, are the best sources of children's books in English. Used and new bilingual or Spanish books are more challenging to find, mostly through amazon.com

Blankies of various kinds are paired with these books. They come from thrift stores and private donations. We prefer the all-cotton or flannel blankets with satin trim. Baby quilts are also donated by three different quilting clubs: Outlaw Quilters (Darla Drain); Mount Cross Quilters (Marilyn Gardner); and Ojai Church of Christ's Comfort Quiltmakers/Project Linus (Teresa Perry and Robin Garretson).

In the past few weeks my Westmont College roommate (1968), Susie Whitmore Minyard, mailed us twenty-five crocheted baby afghans to go with the books.

LEVEL 3

LOVE & BELONGING: RECEIVING AFFECTION, GIVING AFFECTION, TRUST & FRIENDSHIP

Photo by a friend

52

WATER HOSPITALITY

Nearly every time we visit families, they offer us bottles of water. Maybe because of their own experiences with unsafe water, most fieldworker families buy 4-, 8- and 12-ounce bottles of water by the case. It is always on their shopping lists.

For families who live close to a source of reverse osmosis or bottled water or can easily get to a grocery store, we have provided a 3- or 5-gallon refillable water jug which is much more economical. However, if they have to walk to the grocery, with children and a stroller, those jugs are heavy and impractical.

Recently we have started offering Pur water faucet filters to families. The cost of the device is approximately $25 and a box of three replacement filters for $28. It will take up less space than water bottles, and always be available in the kitchen. Plus it saves on the environment. So far, our families are satisfied with this option.

This takes me back to the gifts fieldworkers give their guests. Another popular gift for visitors are containers of the fresh fruit (strawberries, raspberries, blueberries) they just picked at work. These are a delicious treat.

One woman I visit shares the freshly cooked, still hot chayote squash she grows in her tiny garden. It's known to be an excellent source of Vitamin C, manganese and antioxidants. To me chayote tastes like a cross between a potato and zucchini with the consistency of cooked summer squash. It's delicious with butter, lemon pepper and garlic salt.

53

THANK YOU NOTES

I've tried to instill in my own children the need to show appreciation to people who do kind things for us. It's a social grace that makes all the difference in the world in interpersonal relationships. Part of our family folklore is the time we had a Charlie Brown Christmas tree with three presents under the tree for each family member. To extend the opening of presents, we wrote thank you notes after each one. It's a story that brings lots of laughs to this day.

Many people have donated money, time and services to our families. I encourage them to write thank you notes. Sometimes I've provided the stationery, stamps and addresses for that purpose. It is a foreign concept to many. Gratitude does come in smiles, non-verbal signs and eventually, in the development of trust. Meanwhile, we do things because we care or because they are needed, not for thanks.

54

AMOR DE ABUELO BUSY BAGS

For children having to wait with their parents in line at doctor's offices or other agencies, Alexis and her sister also created "Busy Bags" with little boxes of raisins, mini water bottles, little cars, dolls, stuffed animals, small coloring book and crayons. Goldfish crackers. These "Amor de Abuelo" bags (Grandpa's Love, as we called them) also were given to First Five for the children who come to their classes with their parents.

55

ALE PURSES

Alexis O'Neill, an acquaintance of mine through a writing organization, SCBWI (Society of Children's Book Writers and Illustrators) took it upon herself, enlisting her sister, Barbara Veazey's help, to create two dozen or more of these special purses. They were distributed though First Five and another organization that work with women in transition. For whatever reason, but often spousal abuse, women find themselves and their children in shelters or other facilities for their protection. These purses are designed to provide practical and comfort items for this part of their journey.

Large purses or small duffel bags are filled with small versions of many or all of these items:

blanket & pillow
toothbrush and toothpaste
hairbrush/comb
tampons or pads
Chapstick
Band-Aids
shampoo & conditioner combination
flashlight
2-3 stamped envelopes
Kleenex
sanitizer wipes
bar of soap in container
scarf
socks
towel

hand lotion
hand sanitizer
snacks (protein bars, nuts, fruit juice boxes, beef jerky, dried fruit,
lifesavers or hard candy)
laundry soap
roll of quarters
deodorant
washrag
note of encouragement
pen and pad of paper
2-3 quart-sized baggies
nail clippers/file
small pair of scissors
night shirt
plastic baggies can be used to organize the items by use.

Alexis and Barbara were able to get some items donated from local stores and purchased the rest at a 99 Cent Store or drugstore. The purses came from thrift stores or were donated by friends.

ALE Purses stands for Alexis and for Atomic Love Explosion, a phrase born in one of our earliest Abundant Table Church gatherings. I thought this small, powerful gesture might start one of those. Alexis, you and your sis started something!

56

DOLLS

I keep my eyes open for baby dolls that just need a little clean-up and some new clothes. Baby dolls of all colors. Sometimes I find new ones on sale at Target or other department stores that I can't pass up. Many little children enjoy playing with them but often have younger siblings who fill that need.

Sometimes when there is a new baby in the household, I will take a doll and doll furniture for the youngest child in the family to play with when the new mom is caring for the newborn.

57

PHOTO COLLECTIONS

Another hobby of mine is taking pictures. I have hundreds of photos of farmworker families and their children on my computer. After the fires when the families lost what photos they had, I took pictures, enlarged and framed them and gave them as gifts to the family.

It is always a joy to receive text messages with photos from families. And they come in very handy when a family wants to tell us their sick child is back in the hospital or their child has gotten an award at school or whatever news. One child in the hospital set me up with Snapchat so we could communicate during his hospitalization.

My goal is to create a photo album or framed collage for each of the families we work with when one or more of their children goes off to college. It is to remind them of what beautiful people they are, the fun times they had together and how much they are loved.

58

ROCKING CHAIRS

For two new moms and a family with a sick child, I felt that they must have rocking chairs. And as always happens in these cases, shortly I found them in a thrift store or at the end of a yard sale. After painting them and making them look like new, I delivered them to the families. I guess it's a cultural thing. The rocking chair was an indispensable part of my motherhood years and I wanted to share it.

I have also found children's rockers and given them fresh paint and even put Juan Pablo's name on his. Again, it is for comfort and safety.

59

MOM'S CARE ASAP

One of our teens dreamed up this beautiful idea while watching her mom struggle with depression, frustration and exhaustion. We decided to treat her mother to some special pampering. First, we took her to a hairdresser who cut and styled her hair; then for a facial and make-up session, and finally, for a manicure and pedicure. We asked each pampering provider to give her extra love, extra attention since this was her first time for each. The experience made her feel special, loved and honored. It turned out to be the first of many changes in her life over the next two years, including buying herself a new red car and getting her driver's license. I'd like to think she felt worthy of the best and kindest treatment which helped to transform her self-care. And I dream of providing these services and massages for all the people we serve, men and women, reminiscent of *Queen for a Day*.

60

BIRTHDAY BASH

On my 71st birthday this spring, I had a delivery to make to one of our families who was returning to Mexico. I was feeling very sad having watched the parents survive the Oxnard Fire and raise their four beautiful children during their stay in Oxnard. Recently their grandfather was killed in an auto crash in their pueblo. They had just talked with him on the phone before the accident, while they were at our home, coincidentally, and were heart-broken. Their mother suffers some kind of illness that makes her hurt all over. They are terrified that if they stay away any longer, they might miss seeing her again, too.

The young father told me the last time he saw his mother was fifteen years ago, having left Mexico as a teen. He really wanted to see her one more time and to have her meet his wife and children. He knows that the likelihood of them returning to America is very slim because they are undocumented. But their four children (ages 10 to four months) are all American citizens. Their eldest loves school and told us she wants to be a teacher someday.

I was feeling so, so sad about them leaving, knowing that their employment prospects there were very slim. I would miss each of them terribly.

To brighten the mood, I brought a big birthday cake covered in berries. Several family members were there and they all sang to me and we ate birthday cake and chatted away. It will always remain a very happy memory. If they can be hopeful and upbeat in the face of sadness and uncertainty, I want to be that way, too!

61

COMPUTERS, CRIBS & COFFEE

Fieldworker children who attend schools with computer labs or computers in their classroom are taught computer literacy. Few of them, however, are able to have computers of their own until high school or even college.

On two or three occasions, FoF has been able to provide a computer to a student. I would love to make sure all of our families who have children in school and are learning with and about computers, have access to one at home. It allows them to complete homework and other assignments more efficiently. I remember when a high school junior told me she was writing a composition on her phone!

Cribs are not the norm for babies and toddlers of our families. Generally, the entire family sleeps together, in one bed or in one room. We provided at least four families with cribs only to find out later that these were given away or turned into storage. I have noticed some new mothers put their infants in cradles or bassinets. I asked one mother what she needed for her new baby after we'd provided a complete layette. She texted me a picture of a bassinet which was later donated, along with cash and baby blankets, by the local Dem-Moms' Club. She preferred that to the wooden porta crib we'd given her four years ago for her baby girl. I notice a spacing of four-five years (or longer) between children. Therefore, most of their baby items have long-ago been passed on to a relative.

Coffee-drinking is newly-acquired for fieldworkers. I suspect it is seeing the Starbucks on every corner and even in grocery stores that creates the interest in trying coffee drinks. I'm hesitant to mention this because it is not a healthy habit, really. Nor is eating ice cream cones. I am guilty of both.

My own little grandchildren and I went to Starbucks when they were still toddlers. It was our date. They could pick orange or apple juice and we'd ask the barista to make a slushy for them and an iced latte for me and put both in to-go cups. Sometimes we'd sit at a table with our drinks and art supplies and draw pictures. This was all we needed for a date...until they got older and discovered the cake pops!

So, I carry on this grandma-grandchild tradition with my farmworker children. Older ones already know about the fancier blended drinks with whipped cream, but this is a very rare treat.

62

FUNERAL MARIGOLDS

One of our families lost their grandfather to complications of heart disease. This is one of three families who had lost everything but their lives in the Oxnard Fire and experienced severe financial loss. This time of grief added to their load of sadness. My mother was visiting us from Monterey Peninsula and I told her about the family's situation and the funeral going on this evening. She wanted to go with me.

I'd not been to a Mexican funeral before. I didn't know what was appropriate. We stopped at Trader Joe's and got some pots of marigolds which I know have special meaning to Mexicans and are used extensively on *Día de Muertos*, Day of the Dead, Celebration. *The Day of the Dead is a Mexican holiday celebrated throughout Mexico, in particular the Central and South regions, and by people of Mexican heritage elsewhere.*
https://www.nationalgeographic.com/travel/destinations/north-america/mexico/top-ten-day-of-dead-mexico/

Mom and I sat in the back of the church. At the appointed time, she and I went up to the front row to comfort Grandma, her daughter, two granddaughters and grandson. I went up to Grandpa in the open casket and leaned over to say we'd look out for his family.

Afterwards, we went into the parlor and had lemonade, coffee and cake together. It was a meaningful time for my mom and me to share this important and intimate moment with this family. We were the only non-Spanish-speakers there. It reminded me of growing up in

Hawaii and being the only *haole* at an event. It was a familiar and not uncomfortable feeling.

After the Hueneme fire that claimed the life of a young father and his 5-year-old son, there was a funeral mass followed by a service at the cemetery. I went alone to both and again was one of only two or three non-Hispanic mourners. It was terribly sad, especially at the cemetery with two coffins side-by-side, a big one and a smaller one, with the wife/mother going between the two of them. And the toddler daughter crying in her grandmother's arms—whether for her distressed mother or her lost father and big brother.

In times like this, there are just no words. I went the following week to deliver a $1,000 check to help with her expenses. It seemed such a weak gesture in the enormity of the family's loss.

63

HANDMADE QUILTS

I have always loved quilts. Especially Amish quilts, which are stitched mostly by hand. There is a quality of awe to a blanket put together, piece by piece, stitch by stitch. The colors are chosen carefully and the design is very deliberate. Even quilts that are quilted by machine.

There's an old Pillsbury jingle that says, *Nothin' says lovin' like somethin' from the oven*. Well, to me, nothing says love like a quilt. Each finished product that goes to a person says, *You are special. You are worth the time, energy, skill and money I put into this to keep you warm and protected for many years to come and maybe to give as a keepsake someday.*

And so, to the quilt-makers who have donated your creations to our fieldworkers, I owe a special thank you.

64

CARE PACKAGES

For our students in college, it's fun to send a little package of goodies during midterms and final exams. Some of the suggested items are anything chocolate: bars, kisses, covered popcorn or pretzels. Cracker Jacks, Taquis chips, peanuts in their shells, tamarind candy, red licorice sticks, and breakfast bars. Fruit nectar drinks and juice boxes. It's also good to pack in a little greeting card that says something like "I'm thinking of you. Best wishes for successful exams. I believe in you."

For an added bonus, stick in a gift card to Starbucks, Dunkin Donuts, Subway or Target.

65

LOVE NOTES

Notes and pictures received from children are one of my most prized possessions. They stay on the refrigerator, cupboard doors and in a special file that I can go back to for a quick picker-upper.

When I taught school many years ago, I was always delighted by the way children are so easily able to put their feelings on paper—in words, in drawings—and how generous they are with love and thanks. My own children will tell you that I was a fanatic about thank you notes. (See #53, Thank You Notes.) Being thankful is a good trait, right? And it doesn't have quite the effect when you have to ask for it.

Over the years, I've learned to recognize appreciation in other ways. For example, when children have a little bit of spending money to use as they wish at the Farmer's Market during Farm Camp, they nearly always save out some (or all) for a gift for their mom. And something for their siblings at home.

When you give children paper, crayons and pencils, they often create "little treasures" or love notes for the adults in their life. Our little ones do the same. I think one of the most precious notes I've received was from a 9-year-old who drew a picture of her family, our dogs and Ted and me. Her words were "I am so glad you are in my life." Priceless.

66

INDEPENDENCE DAY

One Christmas season a family asked us for bikes for their four children, ages nine to thirteen. Friends of Fieldworkers put the word out to some supporters and we raised the money to buy the bicycles and helmets to go with them. It was such a happy moment to see the children seeing their own wheels for the first time. They wanted to head directly to the park to ride.

67

BUBBLES & BALLS

A very easy way to entertain children in a small living room or in a park is to throw around balls. Nerf balls or blow-up plastic ones are the best in small spaces. Rubber balls and leather soccer balls are great for chasing around in larger ones.

Bottles of bubbles are also a perfect way to entertain or engage children. These are great things to have in the car when visiting families. The 99 cent Store and Dollar Tree have both for about $1 each. Balls and bubbles are very inexpensive but can provide hours of pleasure for children.

68

CHRISTMAS SHOPPE

Low income parents everywhere struggle at Christmas time. They see and hear of all the wonderful toys and things available for children, but not for their own children. The holidays can be a sad time for them if they are unable to provide gifts for their loved ones.

ACTION of Camarillo holds annual Christmas Shoppes in two or more locations (Oxnard, El Rio). It is a gala event for the whole family. Children are entertained with food, games and art projects while their parents shop for new gifts for their children. Each church hall is packed with tables full of toys and items for all ages of children. There is free gift wrapping available. Sometimes, these are the only gifts under their trees, so this is an exciting event for all.

ACTION mobilizes churches, businesses and volunteers to support families through nonprofit organizations. Each late November and early December Friends of Fieldworkers, Inc., is asked how many invitations we need. This year we requested 35 and we shared ten of these with another organization serving fieldworkers. The rest were hand-delivered to our families. They went on a specific day and time, receiving gift tickets at the door based on the size of their family. And then the fun begins. This brings joy to the children and their parents.

LEVEL 4

ESTEEM: RESPECT FOR ONESELF, DESIRE FOR RESPECT FROM OTHERS DIGNITY, ACHIEVEMENT, MASTERY

Feliz Navidad and a peaceful, safe and a love-filled New Year in your new shoes!

From all your Friends of Fieldworkers

69

CHRISTMAS SHOES

Most of our children only have one pair of shoes. Children only get another pair when the existing one is worn out. When asked what they'd like for their children for Christmas, if they could get one thing, parents almost invariably ask for shoes. For five years now, we have ordered Payless

Shoes Gift Cards and given them out, one gift card per member of the family. The company gave us a 10% discount when we bought them in October. We could pay over two months. In 2018 we purchased 111 X $35 cards and gave them out 100 to our families. We shared eleven with another organization for their families. The families often are able to go to a Payless Shoe sale and buy two or three pairs with each card. Unfortunately, this company went out of business in 2019, so we are seeking a new shoe store in the area.

70
PERSONAL STORIES

Invisible Woman by Roxie Ray, www.RoxieRay.com, photo
by W. Scott Miles, scott@TheScientificPhotographer.com

One of my dreams for Friends of Fieldworkers is to collect stories from our fieldworkers and to publish them in a book. Our earlier attempts have not been very successful. We need to know what our families' lives were like before we met them; then, in the transition to America; and now, since they've been here. The reasons are many but the top three are these:

1) to know their history and life experiences to increase our understanding of and compassion for them.

2) To learn what their true needs and heartfelt desires are for themselves, their children and grandchildren.

3) To share with the world their stories for better understanding, appreciation and valuing of their contribution to our society.

And we want all of this gathered information to better inform what we do to be the best friends and supporters we can possibly be to them. We don't want our values, desires and needs to clash with theirs. This is not about us; it's about them!

71

A SAD GOODBYE

This was a surprise to me. I had no idea how hard it would be to say goodbye to one of our families whom we'd known since 2013. Two brothers, their wives and four children moved into an apartment together after they were displaced by the fire. Three children were born to the younger brother's family. We'd watched them all grow up and shared meals, work days, farm camp days and Christmas cookie baking days.

Their two-bedroom, one bath apartment saw a lot of life with birthday parties, welcome home-baby days, and no-special-reason visits.

A few months ago, while the brothers helped us in our yard, the cousins and I spent the day roasting vegetables, baking a chicken and cookies. I noticed that the men were on their cell phones quite a bit which I'd never seen before. It turns out that their father in Mexico kept calling them to talk about random things. At the time they thought it was rather unusual. The next morning, on his way to an errand, their dad was in a fatal car accident. The family was devastated, of course. Their father was gone. And their mother is ill in Mexico. Of the five brothers in California, the youngest one would take his wife and four children (ages 6 months to nine years old) back to Oaxaca to be with their mother. He hadn't seen her in fifteen years and was afraid she might die before he saw her again.

The day they flew back to Mexico, there were about twenty family and friends in the apartment saying their goodbyes, hugging, crying and taking photos. It was very emotional. I will very much miss the family. The parents were born in Mexico; the four children were born in Oxnard, California. Short of a miracle, this family won't be able to return to the U.S. together. I can't bear to think of the options. Being a friend of specific fieldworkers can be hazardous, but very worth it.

72

WEARABLE ART

Jewelry is something I rarely see worn by fieldworkers. But then, I don't see them dressed for church, birthday parties or other celebrations, either.

So, like Pretty Things, jewelry can be aesthetically pleasing, even if not worn. It doesn't take up much space either so I love to tuck a watch, necklace, bracelet, hair ribbon or ring in a purse or jacket pocket that we give to the families. I sometimes will refurbish a wooden jewelry box and include a few pieces of jewelry in it for a mom and her daughters. Mexican wearable art is very interesting to me and I wear some that I bought at a Mixteco event. The wearable art is colorful, beaded and lightweight. Lovely.

73

PET ROCKS

One young boy, GL, whom I'd known since the Oxnard fire, didn't seem interested in anything except watching TV, sleeping and occasionally playing basketball in the park. I gave him a half dozen gems and rocks in a nice wooden box. Ted and I were headed on a cross-country trip in our motorhome. I was just learning how to use Instagram and so I found myself picking up more rocks for him on the road at every pitstop. I took pictures of the location and the rock and sent them to him. When we got home, I gave him the whole collection, labeled and in little baggies.

I heard later from his family that the rock collection was an important part of his life. Such a small thing could have a big meaning. The children of three of our families were given doll houses by FoF. Now whenever I find dollhouse people or furnishings, I get them for them and either mail or hand deliver them to the children.

If a child shows interest in a particular book or author, I look for other books by the author. When a child expresses an interest in dinosaurs or trains or caterpillars, I seek related books or items to match her/his interests.

74

PEACE CHAIRS

At the San Diego County Fair, we went by the Design in Wood Exhibition, co-sponsored by the San Diego County Fair 22nd District Agricultural Association and the San Diego Fine Woodworkers Association. Volunteer members of one of the largest woodworking associations in the country make small oak chairs for preschoolers using only 19th century hand tools to shape them. The Association makes fifty chairs each year and these last-a-lifetime gifts are donated to various organizations in the community such as day care centers, schools, hospitals, health clinics, shelters, and other charitable organizations. To date, over 1,700 chairs have been donated.

I signed up for two children's hardwood chairs. After having them labeled "Gift of Friends of Fieldworkers, Inc." by a local trophy shop, I delivered them to the children's librarian at Ray D. Prueter Library in Oxnard.

Another use of chairs is to paint and repurpose them as *peace chairs*. After seeing the Peace Chair website, I bought a sturdy wooden one for $7.50 at Goodwill, and painted it with bright colors, peace signs and words. Then I donated it to my teacher friend, Erynn Smith, at E.O. Green Middle School in Oxnard. Her students use it in their peace and reconciliation circles.

75

GARDENS-IN-A-BOX

We start gardens in containers, raised beds or in the ground in our families' yards. I discovered some herbs and other plants that are favored by people from Oaxaca. *Yerba Santa* is used for making soups and tamales, and for medicinal purposes such as stomachache, headache and fever. Yew, cilantro and mint are other favorites. I delivered and helped assemble three raised 4'x4' garden beds (which I'd helped build in my Ojai Master Gardener's group and then purchased for under $100). We also delivered several bags of compost, soil, plants and garden tools.

In another situation, I delivered plastic or clay pots and soil which could be moved more easily. Besides the food, medicine and color these plants provide, they are a way for farmworkers' children to see how their parents tend the soil and plants—what they do at work!

Children get so excited when their own plants thrive under their care. One seven-year-old brought her science project home from school which involved planting a sunflower seed in a Styrofoam cup. As a retired teacher I am excited but shocked, frankly, when these little potted plants make it home safely. She put hers gently in a sunny spot in the yard, watered and tended it daily and was so proud to show it to everyone: a plant with several sunflowers!

Planting sprouted potatoes, carrots, garlic and onions is also fun. The children see how most anything that sprouts roots will grow into an interesting leafy plant. Amaryllis and other bulbs require so little care but fascinate children and adults with colorful surprises.

76

RECIPROCITY

Working in the nonprofit world with fieldworkers I love, I am learning that we don't always see the effect of much of the work we do. We ask questions about what people need and we try to meet those needs. Many times after delivering items to someone's home, I don't hear about whether the clothes fit, whether they liked the food or if they really wanted the help we gave or not. I just kept asking and giving without expecting anything in return.

77

MOVING ON UP

Fieldwork is no one's dream job. Although some have made peace with it, it's not their first occupational choice. One dear friend of mine has worked caring for raspberries for 19 years. Besides the early hours, long days, low pay and the ripping of her hands-on raspberry thorns, she knows it's still her best option for supporting her family and providing medical insurance.

And that is very fortunate because two of her children were just diagnosed with cystic fibrosis which will require specialized lifetime medical care to some degree. An extremely rare diagnosis in the indigenous population, it does very unfortunately, run in families.

So no, working in the fields, hopefully only lasts a few years. When people do change jobs, male fieldworkers tend to move up to apprenticeships in carpentry, plumbing or other construction work. I know one man who travels 90 minutes a day (roundtrip) 6 days a week to his low-paying construction job because his company works state-wide. He had earlier refused to move with them to San Francisco and leave his family. There are some very hard decisions.

Women sometimes clean houses or work in factories or fast food restaurants. Those who move into higher-paying jobs learn English and take risks in applying for jobs in food service, childcare or the rare companies that hire undocumented employees.

What I've noticed is that the people I work with put all their eggs in one basket. Their children. They get them to school every day and believe that their only way out of poverty is in the lives of the next generation. They are not <u>always</u> right, but <u>often</u> are. And that's why we put so much emphasis on education.

78

ROADSIDE ART

John Cerney's Field Art in Salinas, California, and around the world are bigger-than-life painted wood figures of fieldworkers. I first saw them when I lived in Salinas many years ago. They are found along highways 101 and 68 and reflect the importance of the fieldworkers to the economy of Monterey County. It would make sense then, that we commission John Cerney to create pieces of art for our farms along the highways in our area.

When I spoke with him on the phone, John said he can get a photo from us and create a figure from that or he can provide it for us. He does the work in his studio in Salinas and transports and installs it where we want it. We'd have to get permission from the farmer owners, of course. Each art piece, installed, is somewhere around $4,500. It's a startling, powerful image in any field of crops, a reminder of who labors there.

79

MONOGRAM POWER

I learned of a young woman whose sister struggled with addictions and was unable to care for her baby daughter. She got permission from the court to take Bella to her own home and care for her. She was just starting out and had nothing to care for a baby.

Friends of Fieldworkers provided baby clothes of ascending sizes, bottles, blankets, shoes, a playpen and highchair. I'd bought a lovely cross-stitched baby blanket top for under $5 years ago that I was saving... for her, I guess, someone special. A friend I met at the Ojai Ben Franklin Store in the fabric and notions department, Marty McMillan, offered to help. I asked if she would make this into a proper baby quilt and embroider *Bella* in the middle, which she did.

Marty also sewed satin on the edges of several baby blankets for our Blankies and Books project and the name and decorations on two other babies' onesies. This idea came to me from a friend in Albuquerque who stitched *Lorelei* and little flowers on a onesie for my own premature baby girl. I saved it until she had her own baby. This is one more way to recognize individuals and their specialness.

80

HOME BUSINESS

JA has an exceptionally green thumb. Everything she plants grows, from seed, bulb, corm or slip. She brought a piece of Yerba Santa, an all-purpose herb, here to Oxnard, from her mother's garden in Oaxaca. In the little yard in front of their apartment, JA and her husband, RA nurture Yerba Santa and chayote vines, strawberries, mint, vegetables and baby fruit trees.

I got the idea of helping her make a little extra cash to supplement their income. I purchased some Yerba Santa plants in five-gallon pots for $10 each. Whenever I visited a family with a spot for a spreading plant, I offered them one. Yerba Santa can be eaten in a salad, soup, tamales or brewed in a tea for headache, fever or stomachache. It is a comfort plant, much like spearmint or chamomile, reminding people of home, much like in *The Tale of Peter Rabbit*.

I also approached grocers and nurseries in Ojai, Port Hueneme and Oxnard to see if they could sell them to their customers, either as a bundle of cut leaves or in their original nursery pots. Out of 100 pots I bought over the years, we sold two or three. Green's Nursery of Oak View generously provides five-gallon pots and bags of composted potting soil at a discount or free for this project.

81

BIRTHDAY PARTIES

Three birthday parties are memorable. One was for an eleven-year-old boy whose request for dinner was spaghetti and strawberry-topped cake. The family had just moved into a little apartment after the fire and they couldn't afford to put on a party. So we got busy and made a list together. They invited their aunts, uncles and cousins over for this special celebration.

We had lots of excitement and balloons, and presents for all the children, including the birthday boy's favorite Legos. His mom and I prepared spaghetti and a large green salad in the kitchen. We had bottled soda, water and a bowl of fruit.

AR wanted a strawberry cake which I thought was awesome since both of his parents worked in the strawberry fields. I made a box mix in an oblong pan and covered it in vanilla frosting, large halved strawberries and candles.

We ate in the living room balancing plates on our laps or TV trays, watching the kids with their toys. We sang happy birthday and watched the candles being blown out. Then we took lots of photos which I promised to blow up and put in frames since they'd lost all of theirs in the fire.

Another birthday party was for a thirteen-year-old girl whom I'd known since she was seven. My cousin Colette had sent me money from Germany so this young lady could have a special cake. When she visited us a couple of years ago in California, I'd taken her to meet this wonderful family in Port Hueneme and they welcomed her like a queen.

I tried to simply drop off her cake on that afternoon, but her mom insisted that I stay for a special dinner in her honor. And so, that evening we all converged at a neighborhood park and ate delicious barbeque, salad, and tortillas. While the parents prepared the meal and more and more relatives came after work with the cousins, I played with the kids on the jungle gyms, slides, swings and climbing bars. I took photos and played like a kid.

After the barbeque, it was time for cake. The candles had trouble staying lit in the wind but the children didn't mind. This was high drama. They knew something I didn't know. One of the dads turned up his phone and played a Mexican song and everyone joined in. Then, two of the other children pushed the birthday girl's face into the cake. I was shocked and questioned the wisdom of eating cake someone's face had been in. But when I saw her face lit up from behind the frosting and the joyous laughter of everyone, I gave up any hygienic concerns and joined the fun. That was a stellar, unforgettable moment.

And, the third birthday party was my own, celebrated amid the bon voyage event.

82

BLOCKS, LEGOS AND LINCOLN LOGS

Whenever I see these toys on sale, I snatch them right up: wooden blocks, Legos and Lincoln Logs. They are usable over and over again for different kinds of creative projects. Most of the time these are gently/moderately used and I take them home, wash and dry them and use mineral oil on the wooden blocks to restore their natural beauty. I do the same for wooden cars, trains and trucks.

I always include a good plastic tub or container, preferably with a lid so the items can be easily gathered and stored. I always have to keep in mind the youngest member of the family to avoid safety hazards.

If these toys are not used by the children or if they are too much clean-up for the parents, they may be passed on to a friend or relative. I just have to prepare myself for that event and let it go.

83

BIRTHDAY MAIL

Receiving mail is a big deal...for any kid. But for those who have possibly never received a birthday card, it is especially fun. Our friends Dr. KuanFen Liu and her daughter, Terilyn, wanted to volunteer. They came with me on some visits to families to deliver food and other things. They did something else that took quite a bit of time and cash to brighten our fieldworkers' days:

A high school student, BH, made a calendar of all our peoples' birthdays. Terilyn (11) and her mom made or bought birthday cards and filled them with either $5 (for kids) or $10 (for adults) bills and mailed them out over the period of a year. That was 50+ cards and bills. I would love to have seen those happy faces.

Other people have helped with this project, but no one as consistently as KuanFen and Terilyn.

84

WEED MONEY

When the children visit, we have a game where they get a penny per weed that they pull in the yard. They keep count. There aren't many ways that they can earn money so even if it's just a dollar or two, they're into it.

Actually, they really are good workers and help their parents without much cajoling, especially with the younger children. Helping each other is just expected and part of their culture.

85

TREASURED GIFTS

I love the pictures and notes our children write. That's why I collect computer paper, copy paper, scrap and lined paper, any kind of paper. And especially the art board left over in picture-framing shops. Envelopes, colored pens and pencils of all sorts. Stickers, stamps and stamp pads. Children love to create with any kind of paper and writing tools, paints and brushes.

Children can draw, write stories, letters, notes to their friends and parents, make collages and paintings, do their homework, practice their math tables and all kinds of other projects.

Some of my most treasured gifts from children are the notes they write me and the pictures they draw. I will include a couple in this book. I post them on cupboards, on the refrigerator in frames and in a folder marked, "Treasures."

Drawn by PV and MP.

LEVEL 5

COGNITIVE: KNOWLEDGE, UNDERSTANDING, CURIOSITY, PREDICTABILITY, EXPLORATION, NEED FOR MEANING

86
CRADLE LITERACY

As mentioned earlier, one of my hobbies is collecting children's books, especially award-winning ones with beautiful illustrations and good writing. Not preachy, how-to, "educational series" type books.

I find books at Friends of the Library used book stores, thrift stores, yard sales, especially at-the-end-of-the-day sales. Second Helpings and New to You Thrift Stores in Ojai sell children's books for 50 cents each. Goodwill sells them for 79 cents and on 50% off Wednesdays, 40 cents.

On two recent trips to Cos Cob, Connecticut, to visit our family, we just happened to be there for their annual library parking lot book sale. I explained to the head librarian our project in California for fieldworkers' children. He gifted us with several boxes of children's library-bound books at the end of the day. We shipped them all home to

Ojai in priority mail boxes, figuring that each beautifully-bound book cost about 50 cents, including shipping.

I ask every family I visit if they'd like their very own library-in-a-box for their home. I deliver a colored milk crate or wooden bookcase ($5-10) full of children's books. Some are in Spanish; most are in English. Board books are for the babies and toddlers; picture books and early readers for the school-aged children and chapter books and young adult literature for the older children. Because of the cost of housing, food, clothing and other necessities, most of our children have never owned a book. They are a luxury.

Children's books: find them at Friends of the Library shops that many libraries now have (especially at their bi-annual sales). You can get them at reasonable prices at the beginning of the sale, priced by the bag near the end, and free just before they are taken away to Goodwill or a book distributor. Sometimes librarians will save the Spanish children's books for me to pick-up. Garage sales, rummage sales, (ask for left overs), thrift stores, neighborhood on-line announcements (Ojai's Unconditional Give or Take). Bargain.

Once, when I asked two teens if they were enjoying their books, they beamed, "Oh, yes, we keep them safe in a box in the closet!"

87

READING TO CHILDREN

I love to read to children in their home, a book of their choice, even for 10 minutes. It's a very easy thing to do. I find a spot on the couch, a bed, or the floor. I have the child bring me a couple of their favorites and read. Or we take turns reading. It can be a very pleasurable exchange and sets a good example. Older siblings can read to younger ones and new, emergent readers can read to older brothers and sisters. Mom and Dad are usually busy catching up with the house work, cooking, shopping, laundry and other errands on their one day off.

This is the whole point of the Blankies and Books Program, where babies are introduced to colorful picture books holding their favorite blanket in the company of someone who cares about them—a parent, friend, teacher, sibling or other relative. It's priceless time.

Books on CD are also powerful ways to get kids interested in stories, hearing one or more readers read books to them at their age level or possibly two-three levels above. It is particularly good for young children learning English, acquiring language faster than most ever will when older.

88

EARLY CHILDHOOD

After the Oxnard fire in 2013 and having learned of the many children evacuated from their homes, I looked for programs in the community that might offer help to our families. I found the following through which many services for the family could be accessed.

First Five California/ Neighborhoods for Learning

From Oak Park to Oxnard to Ojai, the 11 First 5 Neighborhoods for Learning (NFLs) are helping families raise children who are healthy, nurtured, and prepared for kindergarten.

This program resides in some elementary schools, catering to needs of children, 0-5, before they are ready for Head Start. Both are amazing programs. Head Start began in 1964. **Unfortunately, our government is cutting funding to this program in half this year. That means, most of the programs for this age group will be cut-out entirely or re-modeled with fewer teachers and resources. It's shameful.**

Here's more general information from their websites:

<u>California Head Start</u> (benefits.gov)

A Federal program that promotes the school readiness of children from birth to age five from low-income families by enhancing their cognitive, social, and emotional development. Head Start programs provide a learning environment that supports children's growth in many areas such as language, literacy, and social and emotional development. Head Start emphasizes the role of parents as their child's first and most important teacher. These programs help build relationships with families that support family well-being and many other important areas.

Many Head Start programs also provide <u>Early Head Start</u>, which serves infants, toddlers, and pregnant women and their families who have incomes below the Federal poverty level.

<u>Early Head Start (EHS)</u> programs serve infants and toddlers under the age of 3, and pregnant women. EHS programs provide intensive comprehensive child development and family support services to low-income infants and toddlers and their families, and to pregnant women and their families.

1-866-763-6481 (program locater)
http://www.first5california.com
http://www.ccfc.ca.gov
http://www.first5ventura.org
https://www.cbo.gov

At of this writing, I am not aware of the government's plans for Head Start.

89

BRIBERY

My son struggled with reading until he was in third grade. During the summer between second and third grade, I bribed him. The summer before I had offered him a penny a page. This time I offered him three times as much. By the end of summer he was reading books with a flashlight under his bedcovers. And his first whole book was an adult novel, *The Power of One*, by Bryce Courtenay. Of course, I took the credit. When he was ready, he started reading on his own and is an avid reader to this day.

I learned many years later in graduate school that a child's brain must be "myelinated" (a kind of hormonal marination) before he/she is capable of the complicated skills of reading. And yet we suspect kindergarteners of having learning disabilities when they can't recognize their ABC's and read basic primers. We test, diagnose and place them in special classes before their brains are even ready to perform the complicated right and left brain communication which allows reading to occur.

As a retired reading and special education teacher, I believe in early intervention, the earlier the better. But not being ready to read before third grade, by itself, doesn't warrant concern. Other behaviors have to be present involving language, small and large muscle coordination, social adjustment, vision or hearing, signs of aggression or anxiety, or irregular patterns of concentration. Children of three languages—Spanish, English and Mixtec (or other indigenous language)—may take a bit longer to process the language spoken around them and to them. This is normal behavior.

However, if children have no physical reasons for not reading, they may just not be motivated to do so. They may not have any books at home. They may not have a quiet spot to read them. However, that doesn't mean we shouldn't try. Provide books at an early age. If they don't attempt to read because they don't see the point, well, in that case, try bribery. I pay school-aged children to read books to themselves or board books to their younger siblings. They keep a list of titles and a 1-sentence summary. I pay them by the page. It sometimes works.

90

EARNING GOOD GRADES PAYS

Three birds with one stone. It's a way for children who have very few ways to earn money to do so. And at the same time, they are given an incentive to earn good grades. At the end of each semester, children mail or text us a copy of their grades. They can be provided with self-addressed, stamped envelopes to make it easier.

Each A is worth $5; each B is worth $3 and each C, $1. It is a bit more complicated for elementary children whose grades are numbers, 1-5, in many categories. We'll figure it out.

Ventura County Credit Union opens free minor's savings accounts for our children. MP is nine years old and was asked to sign her first check and hand it to the bank employee for depositing: $100 and $25 for her grades. The credit union only requires $5 to open any account, checking or savings but we wanted to start hers with a flourish. From now on, FoF will transfer money to her education account or send a check for her to deposit.

So far, we have gotten written permission for ten children to open accounts. We may also look for donors to match what the children earn, thereby making good grades even more attractive. Of course, the ultimate goal is to hook kids on learning and to be proud of their achievements.

Another part of this plan is to get written consent to contact the children's teacher(s) to discuss their achievement in school, their report cards and discuss ways to improve their school experience. We found two Mixtec-speaking employees at Oxnard School District, Argelia Alvarado and Norma Zarate, who are liaisons between parents and school. They are very anxious to work with us on behalf of the students.

The report cards are even difficult for <u>me</u>, a retired teacher, to understand. They use words like *bridging* and *expanding* in describing a child's ability to understand and use English language. In math, they use *operations and algebraic thinking* and *geometry*. I can see how such report cards are hard or impossible for parents with little education to interpret.

Walking to the Next Field by Roxie Ray, www.RoxieRay.com

91

ADULT SCHOOL

Many of our parents would love to go to school here if given the chance. But since they work six days a week, they only have one day to do the laundry, housework and to be with their children or relax a little. A favorite pastime is going to the park where the children can run and play after being in school and tight quarters all week.

For those students who are able to attend them, Ventura County has some impressive educational programs: high school diploma, high school equivalency, adult basic education, career technology education, ESL and citizenship classes. And these programs are free or very reasonably priced.

Persons able to overcome obstacles of childcare, work exhaustion and finances, can attend school to improve their knowledge and chances of a better job than working in the fields—a dream of many immigrants.

92

WORM BIN

One day three children came over to our house and spent the day with me. One of the projects we did together was building a worm bin in a Rubbermaid bucket with a lid. We drilled a dozen holes in the bottom and a dozen in the top. We tore pieces of newspaper into thin strips and filled one half of the bucket with them. We added some crunched-up egg shells, coffee grounds, cut-up salad greens and fruit scraps from the kitchen. We covered that up with more paper scraps to within 4 inches of the top. We sprayed all with water to create a damp, not soggy habitat. Then we dug up two cupsful of worms from our garden and gently put them into their new home.

I explained to the children how to keep the worm bin going in their apartment if their parents gave their approval. Or, to take it to the fourth-grade classroom where they are studying soil.

After two months, these worms had created the most beautiful black gold soil. There was no bad smell. The kids were thrilled and able to take their worm bin to Summer Farm Camp a few weeks later. It was a very proud moment.

93

COLLEGE SCHOLARSHIPS

Our goal for years has been to endow a college scholarship fund at CSU Channel Islands for academically-qualified children of fieldworkers. It would take an endowment of over a million dollars in order to pay for the tuition of one student every year. While we look for that cash, we have another alternative.

House Farmworkers! annually awards four $2,000 college scholarships to qualified students. We are now donating money to them to extend it to five.

We additionally will help a student whose family we work with already, if they have a need for assistance. Because local community colleges provide tuition and fee scholarships to first generation farmworkers' children, they mostly need help with their books.

94

VILLAGERS

Roanna Prell and I sat at the dining room table of our high school student, B.H, and her mother. Roanna came as a mentor to B.H. who was about to enter U.C. Berkeley, the university where her own daughter graduated from. Roanna gave B.H. some very wise advice for nearly an hour.

The three things I remember the most were these. First, be understanding of and patient with herself that she was entering into a completely foreign world of academia in the fast track. While she had been at the very top of her high school graduating class, she would be surrounded by and competing with the top students from many other schools. Little fish in big pond.

And, two, her college classes should always come first if she's to survive there. She should definitely not take a job in her first and maybe second year at Berkeley. Roanna personally would add to her other college scholarships and grants to keep her solvent in school. All she asked for was some kind of list, showing her budgeted needs and resources.

And three, she needed to remember that she is not alone. She has a village here at home (and close to her school, the Encampment for Citizenship) that she could always rely on. And we are all here for her.

Roanna has continued for two years to keep in contact with our student in college, giving her encouragement and covering her budgetary shortfall. She is a God-send.

LEVEL 6

AESTHETIC: APPRECIATION AND SEARCH FOR BEAUTY, BALANCE & FORM

95

KIDS' PROJECTS

Bring children home and do projects together. Paint a chair; make a magazine picture collage; bake Christmas cookies with cookie cutters; do watercolors or other artwork (local art framing shops are happy to donate scraps of their materials that make perfect painting material); pick fruit; do simple cooking lessons such as how to stuff a chicken with oranges and lemons and bake. Or how to roast vegetables or make fresh-picked, fresh-squeezed orange juice. Collecting, washing and cracking fresh eggs is a favorite. Sometimes I provide plain card stock and envelopes (from Michael's) which the children decorate. Then they dictate to me a thank you note to someone and copy it on their card. We address and stamp it and explain the importance of saying *thank you.*

96

FARM CAMP

For the past four summers, Ted and I provided transportation for our farmworker children, ages 5-13, to the Abundant Table's Farm Camp. It is held at the McGrath Family Farm site in Camarillo, the North Oxnard United Methodist's Community Roots Garden and the Farmer's Market of Downtown Oxnard. Vern Norstrup makes sure our children are given a scholarship every year.

We picked up 8-10 eager campers in our motorhome for five days each summer and delivered them to those locations. They spent each day learning about plants, insects, soil, composting, earthworms (their favorite!), planting, harvesting and eating produce. At McGrath Family Farm they observed and fed farm animals—turkeys, chickens, lambs, goats, pigs and homing pigeons.

On Thursdays each summer we went to Oxnard Farmer's Market and each child was given $10 for spending money. Their instructions were to buy at least one fruit, one vegetable, and something else of their choice. Many of the children bought gifts for their mothers or siblings at home. JR bought an orchid plant which still blooms in their living room window three years later. If they really wanted an item but were short on cash, I taught them to bargain, which often worked.

This summer, we and the children were especially blessed to be part of the Encampment for Citizenship's annual encampment held for 3 1/2 weeks on the CSU Channel Islands' campus. Friends of Fieldworkers and The Abundant Table hosted a service-learning experience for five of EFC's students. At the Farmer's Market they ate, shopped, ran and played together. The end of camp was marked by our annual trip to Coldstone for a sweet treat.

Linda Quiquivix (QuiQui), from The Abundant Table created her own special treat at Cold Stone Creamery with spearmint from the Farmer's Market, coffee ice cream and powdered cinnamon sticks.

Another addition to this summer's camp was a trip to the Santa Barbara Zoo. Eight campers and four adults had a memorable time seeing the animals, riding the zoo train, participating in the dinosaur show and spending their $10 each in the Zoo Store.

In addition to the lessons about beauty, conservation, recycling, care for the earth, planting and harvesting techniques, cooking, biology and agriculture, the children had the time of their lives, out in the sun, being loved by their teachers. For most of them, this is the highlight of their summer and the only time they don't have to stay inside at home or with a sitter while their parents work six days a week. Every child I've asked preferred school to vacation.

97

FAMILY FIELD TRIP

Over Easter Vacation this year we went to the Santa Barbara Zoo for the annual *El Día del Niño* (Day of the Child). Our dear friends, PV and BP, their little boy (1 1/2) and girl (9) and I spent the day together exploring the great assortment of wild animals. The Santa Barbara Zoo is a favorite of mine because of the closeness of the animals and the wild nature of the enclosures. When we got there, I carried on one of our family traditions. Each family member got an envelope with "love money" in it to spend anyway they wanted at the zoo.

Later, when we talked on the phone, in the words of their young daughter, *Something fun at the zoo was that we were walking together to go look at the giraffes and then we fed them lettuce. We were all together feeding the giraffes at one time. It was fun watching the flamingos and we took pictures of many animals. I took pictures of the ducks and the fox, the turtle and the penguins.*

I even saw an elephant and two bunnies and a blue bird. His hair was up like he had gel in his hair. Then we saw ducks in the duck pond, splashing and scratching like they were taking a bath. And then we watched one duck rescue a duck by telling another duck to get off his back...

98

POTTED SUNSHINE

At our little Fruit N Stuff Stand in front of our house, we place several potted plants at a time. I plant cuttings that I get from numerous sources—including my daughter's home in Santa Monica. Succulents are plump and healthy in the sun and moisture from the sea. I have an entire section of my garden called the Korneychuk Garden which overflows with succulents I helped daughter Jennie's gardener prune.

The plants are for sale for $1 to $10 depending on the size. I often take some of these plants when I visit a family. Many of them have green thumbs and enjoy an added member to their collection.

Some of my favorite plants to grow are amaryllis bulbs and sweet potato vines. These bring life to a dinner table and conversation.

99

PRETTY THINGS

Most of our families are living with the absolute bare necessities... for cooking, sleeping, cleaning and dressing for school and work. And so I make it a point to include something pretty mixed in with other more practical things.

Some of these are China tea cups and saucers, wicker fruit baskets, scented candles, a fancy doily and colorful table cloths. Crystal or other fancy vases filled with fresh lavender or my garden flowers are popular. As are colorful tins that hold perfumed soap.

Pretty clothing might be a very soft hand-crocheted scarf, colorful underwear or sweater. For men it could be a pair of kid leather work gloves or colorful wool socks. For children, baby dolls dressed in pretty clothes are popular as are freshly stained and oiled wooden cars. For babies my favorite pretty things are soft, two-sided flannel blankets trimmed in matching satin and labeled, "Made with Love."

For one of our young men who was staying in a mobile home we provided a painting of a scene in Mexico to hang on his wall to remind him of his faraway home.

LEVEL 7

SELF-ACTUALIZATION: REALIZING PERSONAL POTENTIAL, SELF-FULFILLMENT, GROWTH

100
PAY IT FORWARD

I absolutely loved that movie about the book, *Pay It Forward*. We have this saying on our bedroom wall. When people say things like, *thank you so much for ___. How can I repay you?* I always say to them, *What has been given to me, I give to you. Now what you have been given, give to others.*

A year ago, one of the young teens whose family was in the Oxnard Fire of 2013 and lost everything they owned, had a baby girl. She's twenty-one now and married. Their baby daughter was born prematurely, weighing under three pounds. Mother, baby and sometimes Dad, spent much of the first three months in two different hospital NICUs. In Ventura and Los Angeles (Children's Hospital).

I was afraid for this baby girl because there were some complications. But now, at nearly a year, she is doing beautifully—a happy and healthy baby.

I talked to her mom shortly after Christmas last year and she told me that she remembered how lonely she got in the hospital NICU, watching over her little one. Worrying, wondering and waiting. Sometimes, even with the hustle, bustle and noise of machines, nurses and babies, she felt alone.

And now that she was home with her family and healthy baby during the holidays, she couldn't help but think of the parents in the NICU this year.

She called to find out how many where there and then she created a dozen little gift bags with items they'd find useful and delivered them to the hospital in time for Christmas. She said that she really wanted *to give back*.

Incidentally, this young mom was the recipient of a library-in-a-box from Friends of Fieldworkers when she was a young teen. In the hospital, there was a new parent's class and at each session she could pick out a baby book for her daughter. By the time they came home together, they had quite a library!

Here is what she requested for her first birthday and got it!

101

FIELDWORKER GOES TO CAL

We met one teen at age 13 who struggled with school and had no real direction in her life. We were getting some compost-rich soil at Community Roots Garden for their family's raised bed garden we provided when we noticed activity at the North Oxnard Methodist Church, where the garden is located. We poked our heads in and saw that someone was telling the young Latino teens of an opportunity to go on a college tour. They could sign up that day. We stayed for the presentation, she signed up and that's how it all started. She began working with the local Tequio Program, with Kim Maxwell Studio's "Find Your Voice" classes, and with Friends of Fieldworkers. We funded dental work for her, and for two years we spent time together in the car going and coming from her appointments in Santa Monica; stopping to try new foods, walking on the beach, shopping and getting acquainted.

She also became very active in a student leadership program called Encampment for Citizenship, traveling to Mississippi, Massachusetts and other cities, mostly by herself. She was further mentored by Kim Maxwell, Ted Lucas, Vanessa Frank, and helped with her college application process by Craig Rosen. Her parents were supportive and a bit reluctant to send her away to the big city.

Today, six years after we first met, she just completed her sophomore year at UC Berkeley, studying pre-law with the goal of becoming an immigration attorney. She lives with a group of 30 other students from somewhat similar backgrounds, learning to cook, collaborate, negotiate and live within their means. In addition, she is very active with the Encampment for Citizenship which had a dramatic impact on her life. This summer she is an intern, leading and encouraging other students as she was a few years ago.

As a junior this fall, she is an R.A. at her collaborative housing, taking a full college load, working on a research project for a stipend and getting excellent grades!

102

A TEEN'S DREAM

I plan on attending university and possibly making a career in law. I really enjoy writing so I have also definitely thought about that as a possible profession. My dream is to go to Stanford (or maybe Brown) to study law and have a successful career. I want to make my parents proud and I really want to give back to my Indigenous community in any way I can, whether it is by becoming a lawyer or sharing my point of view through storytelling. Lately I've been thinking a lot about playwriting because I have found that I love writing in that particular style a lot.

Rarely have I met a 15-year-old who was so focused and sure of where she wanted to go to college and what she wanted to do after graduation. I'm sure I didn't have that level of self-knowledge at that stage of my life. And this special young woman will be the first in her family to go to college.

103

ENCAMPMENT FOR CITIZENSHIP

The Encampment for Citizenship (EFC) develops social justice leaders by providing young people (ages 15-18) of different ethnic, economic, and other backgrounds with a three-week experience in democratic living and working. EFC gives these young activists the tools to address social justice issues in their home communities. In addition, EFC provides an intergenerational network of alumni and friends to support the social justice efforts of recent Encampers.

This organization has had a major impact on our farmworker youth, two I know personally. I could write an entire book on its long-term, far-reaching effect with everyone it touches. Included here is a link to more information about EFC. http://encampmentforcitizenship.org

Ventura County is forever indebted to three people for introducing this program to us this summer on the campus of California State

University Channel Islands. Maria Hernandez, an EFC alumna, is the principal of Rio Real Dual Immersion Academy, a K-8 school focused on language education and the appreciation of cultural contributions by all ethnicities and races. Margot Gibney is the executive director who supports and facilitates the summer program. And, BH, a recent graduate of Hueneme High School, a participant in the EFC program in Mississippi and Massachusetts, and now a pre-law student at University of California, Berkeley. (See #101, *Fieldworker goes to Cal.*) As mentioned earlier, she is an EFC intern this summer, 2019.

Eleanor Roosevelt was Chair of EFC's Board of Sponsors from 1946-62 and was actively involved each summer, inviting Encampers to Hyde Park. Here is a brief description of EFC from *The Eleanor Roosevelt Papers*:

[EFC] was organized as a summer camp "at which young adults of many religious, racial, social and national backgrounds learned the principles and techniques of citizenship in a liberal democracy through lived experience."

104
FIND YOUR VOICE

Kim Maxwell Studio in Ojai is a life-changer for many of us, including me. Kim Maxwell teaches ten-week sessions for adults and for teens where participants develop a community of writers, truth-seekers, voice-developers, performers and friends. Within the walls of this studio all participants are given a safe space to express themselves and explore their experiences for meaning and celebration. We are given time and prompts for free-writes. We are encouraged to go off on our own topic if we have a burning desire. Back in the circle, we may choose to read our writing out loud to our Find-Your-Voice mates and then hear what parts that touched us: what made them laugh, cry or simply, understand. After ten weeks of this intense community work, we perform a 10-15 minute original piece before a live audience of about seventy people, ready to hear and support our stories.

I consider the two ten-week sessions I participated in with Kim Maxwell a kind of soul revival. The sessions were a combination of writing, singing, dancing, speaking, group therapy and Laugh-In.

Kim offers scholarships to the children of fieldworkers for all sessions. Their stories are heart-breaking and passionate. They are full of angst, honest reflection, self-understanding, love and ultimately, hope. Some of our students appear on the Townies' Podcast, created by KMS: *A hometown kind-of-storytelling podcast featuring the original stories of the Ventura County residents who have been in Kim Maxwell's writing & performance class over the last 25 years...All stories were written, performed and recorded at Kim Maxwell Studio in Ojai, CA.*

Sarahi and others [scroll down on the page]:
https://www.thetowniespodcast.org/our-storytellers

Judy and others: https://www.thetowniespodcast.org/our-storytellers/the-townies-ep-32-decisions-decisions

(c) The Townies Podcast 2018

105

FERVENT PRAYER

The following is an experience that left me blessed and renewed in my faith: On the day before his eye surgery, a young father was with his family at home preparing for bed. I called to let him know we were thinking of him, praying for him and a successful surgery and fast recovery. I asked if he'd like us to share a prayer with him over the phone. We both put on our speaker phones. I could hear the family in the background, gathering and getting quieted in their tiny bedroom. And then the most beautiful thing happened.

Each member of the family, in turn, said a prayer for their father and husband, raising their hearts and voices in faith and conviction. I could imagine the angels shushing themselves to listen. And it felt like God himself/herself was present, listening intently to these fervent prayers. I was deeply moved. It was such a sacred moment.

It was indeed a successful surgery though a long recovery. Since then, I have called on the family several times when there was a need in our home or community. When my three-year-old grandson was in the hospital in Connecticut with a severe flu and infection, I asked them to pray. They stopped everything and did so right then. They also said they would pray together with their church family the following Sunday. This is a great gift.

PART II

THE ABC'S OF RUNNING A NON-PROFIT CHARITY ORGANIZATION

The back-story from 1970—Tommy and Maria

My first teaching job was in Chualar, California, a small farming community outside of Salinas. I taught Mexican migrant children ages K-5th grade in a pull-out reading and math program. Mrs. Esther Bird, the principal of the school, would become my favorite principal from all my teaching years. The population of the school was constantly changing, depending on the crops. We were so close to the fields, I could go out the backdoor of my classroom and pick a head of lettuce, cabbage or broccoli that had been missed by the fieldworkers.

I was absolutely charmed by my students and their parents. I even spent some of my weekends painting and trying to cover up the holes in the walls of the little shanties in Camp 21 a couple of miles from our school. It housed many of the fieldworkers and reminded me of a scene in one of John Steinbeck's novels about the Salinas Valley.

One time I took a family to Natividad Hospital (the county hospital) to visit their father and husband. He'd had an aneurism at the age of 32. Who knew those headaches, which did not keep him from working in the fields, would have such a tragic end?

I learned one day of two of my students, Tommy (grade 2) and Maria, (grade 1) leaving school with their mother and three younger siblings on a bus trip to Texas. Their grandmother was dying. I couldn't imagine five children under eight on a bus for two-three days and so I offered to keep Tommy and Maria. We even signed legal guardian papers with the county in case of an emergency.

Those were some of the happiest days of our early lives. My first husband, Kim, and I lived in a tiny one-bedroom apartment over a garage, surrounded by an overgrown lot of plum trees and a struggling vegetable garden. We put the children in our local elementary school in Pacific Grove and prepared for the upcoming holiday like any ordinary family. We went to the beach to swim and play in the sand. We visited the aquarium to watch the seals and sea otters and touch the star fish. We shopped for groceries and had a bedtime routine of baths, books and tuck-ins.

The day before Christmas, the children's mother returned for them. It was a heart-breaking day for us and for them. Their mother soon moved them to the next labor camp, and we didn't see them again for years.

Thirty-five years later I found Tommy and Maria through the Internet. We both discovered that we'd been looking for each other. Maria had even put an ad in a San Francisco paper. Now they lived in Washington; Ted and I lived in California. Since that time, we have seen each other a few times and keep in close touch through Facebook.

This was my first close-up contact with California farmworkers which developed into a life-long love.

Starting a Nonprofit Charity

When we first started helping fieldworkers six years ago, we were able to provide letters of acknowledgment for tax purposes to individuals who gave us items such as furniture, clothing, household items, books, toys, etc., by associating ourselves with nonprofit charities in Ventura County—in particular The Abundant Table and All Saints' Episcopal Church. Before long, however, we were requesting so many letters that it became a burden on them. The only solution we could see was to start our own nonprofit charity.

Initially, we tried to set up the nonprofit ourselves, but soon realized that it would require a lot time and paperwork. There is a ton of documents that need to be created and filed with both the State and the Federal government, and there was no way we could know if we were doing things correctly. So, we decided to have a law firm do all the paperwork for us, and we are glad we did. The law firm we chose specializes in nonprofits and everything was done thoroughly and professionally. We even had our first board meeting in their conference room with a lawyer present. That was the birth of Friends of Fieldworkers, Inc.

Community Partners

These are some of the organizations we have worked with in Ventura County. Sometimes we help them, sometimes they help us, and other times we share our resources.

ACTION (Area Christians Taking Initiative on Needs)
https://www.actionvc.org

To share the love of Christ through acts of service that change lives and strengthen our communities.

CAUSE (Central Coast Alliance United for a Sustainable Economy)
https://www.causenow.org

To build grassroots power to invoke social, economic and environmental justice for the people of California's Central Coast Region through policy research, leadership development, organizing, and advocacy.

CEDC (Cabrillo Economic Development Corporation)
http://cabrilloedc.org

To provide comprehensive housing services and community economic development activities through a community-building approach that facilitates self-sufficiency for individuals and families who are most lacking in opportunity.

CLUE VC (Clergy and Laity United for Economic Justice)
http://www.cluevc.org

To raise the level of awareness among our congregations of the linkage between economic justice and the imperatives of faith and to engage congregations in efforts to influence policy and public opinion to achieve economic justice, particularly for our region's working poor.

Community Roots Garden
http://communityrootsgarden.org

Community Roots Garden is a ministry of the North Oxnard United Methodist Church. Our Garden started in response to hunger issues in Oxnard and a desire to share food and land with those in need.

EFC (Encampment for Citizenship)
http://encampmentforcitizenship.org

Prepares young people to be informed, responsible and effective global citizens through experiential learning and through living in a diverse, democratic community.

Provides youth with a compelling experience in democratic living, with emphasis on critical thinking and social action... to be committed to active citizenship and involvement in their community as justice seekers.

Farmworker Resource Program of Ventura County
https://www.ventura.org/human-services-agency/farmworker-resources/

To build trust and relationships with farmworkers...assist with prompt resolutions to work place concerns...

FoF (Friends of Fieldworkers, Inc.)
http://www.friendsoffieldworkers.org

To befriend and support fieldworkers and their families.

House Farmworkers!
http://www.housefarmworkers.org

To support our agriculture community through City Committees, Farm Worker Immersion, Scholarships, Education and Resources.

IFM (Indigenous Farmworker Study)
http://www.indigenousfarmworkers.org

To describe the size, distribution and language characteristics of this population. The study also provides information on the living and working conditions and the most pressing needs of the indigenous farmworker immigrants.

Lideres Campesinas
http://liderescampesinas.org

To develop leadership among campesinas so that they serve as agents of political, social and economic change in the farmworker community. This leadership has created an organization by and for *campesinas*.

Morgan Thrift
Larry and Tess Morgan ·

To benefit the local Autism Association Chapter.

We teamed up with locally-owned Morgan Thrift Store. When people offered us items we could not use, such as furniture, appliances and instruments, I'd call Larry, the owner. He'd pick up the items in his truck and put them up for sale in their store. Then, when one of our families needed something and if the store had it, they'd get it free.

Ojai Church of Christ Comfort Quiltmakers (Project Linus Blanketeers)
https://www.facebook.com/groups/ojaiquiltmakers/

SCIART (Studio Channel Islands Art Center)
http://studiochannelislands.org/about/who-we-are/

A nonprofit organization dedicated to bringing together artists and community for extraordinary artistic encounters that enrich, educate, and entertain.

SJFVC (Social Justice Fund for Ventura County)
https://socialjusticefundvc.org

The Social Justice Fund for Ventura County promotes fairness, equality and human rights. We strengthen social justice by "creating change, not charity."

TAT (The Abundant Table)
https://theabundanttable.org

Seeks to change lives and systems by creating sustainable relationships to the land and local community.

VCCF (Ventura County Community Foundation)
https://vccf.org

To promote and enable philanthropy to improve our community. For Good. For Ever.

VCOE (Ventura Office of Education) Special Populations Migrant Education
https://www.vcoe.org/Special-Populations

To provide oversight for a number of different programs in school districts within Ventura County. Among the main programs are Cal-Safe, Homeless, Foster Youth Services, Migrant Education, Migrant Education Even Start, Cyber-High online training, Mini-Corps and Migrant Education First Five.

Ventura County Library
https://www.vencolibrary.org

To Inspire our community to explore, discover, and connect.

Board Members

The first Board of Directors meeting of Friends of Fieldworkers, Inc., was held in 2015. Our attorneys told us we are required to have at least three people on our board. Before that day, we spoke to many people about our plans and finally settled on seven board members. We wanted representation from a variety of areas including farming, so we had Judy as President, a local businesswoman as Vice President, and Ted as Treasurer (the three officers your board must have). Our other board members were an Episcopal priest, a college student (child of a farm worker), a farm manager and a farm worker.

During that formative first year, we found it difficult to have regular board meetings because everyone's work schedule was different. We have a smaller board now and it is easier to meet at least twice a year.

If you are thinking about establishing a nonprofit organization, we encourage you to begin with an attorney who specializes in nonprofits. Once your organization is established, you will definitely want the three officers mentioned above on your board, plus a fundraiser, a social media person, and a volunteer coordinator/recruiter.

Fundraising

There are several ways to raise money for a nonprofit. Here are the few ways we have tried so far.

Recreational Yardsales

These raise visibility, not so much cash. One of our teens and my granddaughter offered to help with a yard sale. They tacked up signs in our neighborhood and we emptied the garage of clothes and items donated by Morgan's Thrift Store in Oak View. We had a few oranges from our trees and roadside finds. The girls gave their best sales pitches to the 30 or so people who came by. The cash box had about $37.46 at the end of the long day.

Another time we gathered all manner of items over about a 9-month period of time, loaded them up in our motorhome and delivered them to All Saints' Episcopal Church in Oxnard. We teamed up with the youth of the church and filled the church's social hall with 20 tables of clothes, Christmas and other household items, small appliances, books, shoes, baked goods and plants. We even had an art center for the children.

The day was an unmitigated success for the people who took home large bags of treasures home for a few dollars. It was lots of fun for the local children and created some community goodwill. When we split the profit with the youth group, Friends of Fieldworkers made $300.

Others' yard sales have been a great source of items for us. At the end of a sale, people are usually happy for us to haul everything away. What we can't use for our fieldworkers directly, we can offer at our Fruit and Stuff Stand or give to other organizations.

Gift Card Round-Up

Commonly overlooked resources are unused gift cards. They can be used to purchase almost anything. The most versatile gift cards in our area are for Target, Walmart, CVS, Rite Aid or other drugstores. Grocery gift cards are also helpful if grocery stores that carry Mexican food are nearby, such as Vallarta and El Super in Southern California. If these are not available, paid-up Visa cards can be used most places.

Some gift cards can be cashed in. If not, there might be something of value for fieldworkers. One idea is to have a Gift Card Round-Up Campaign. Send out a request for people to mail all gift cards with some remaining value. Possibly do it around a holiday. Remind them that these may be tax-deductible donations and send a donor letter once the transfer has occurred.

Piggybanks

Besides our own piggy bank on the clothes dryer to capture stray money, we frequently give smaller piggy banks to the children with some coins already in them. We explain that if they find or are given money and they put it in there, they'll be surprised at how fast their money will add up. I actually got this idea from my granddaughter, Kenzie, bless her little heart, who is saving money in her piggy for a motorhome!

Found Money

For as long as I can remember, my father, Glen Fisk, loved to find coins on the ground. Actually, he loved to find golf balls in the Pacific Grove ice plants, coins in pay phones and other "treasures." After he died, finding coins had a new meaning for me. Every time I picked up a coin and saw the words, "In God We Trust," I knew Dad was there with me. All coins found on the ground in pockets or washing machine go into the piggy on the dryer.

A family called right after Christmas and said their father in Mexico was very ill and required special hospital care. Anything we could do to help would be much appreciated. Any amount would go a long way in Mexico. Friends of Fieldworkers' bank account was in the red, and I said that we cared and wanted to help but were low on cash. I could give them our piggy bank, and whatever was in there, they could send home. When they opened the bank there was $94.73, worth about 1,800 pesos!

Sold Gold

Over the past six years, we have been given a fair amount of costume jewelry. I clean it up and put it in little tin boxes or in pockets of purses or even in small jewelry boxes.

Recently we had a very special surprise. In a bag of mixed jewelry given to us by a friend of a friend of fieldworkers (in Northern California), there were some pieces that appeared old. I took them all to a local coin, gold and silver dealer. He carefully looked at each of about 15 pieces of jewelry and after a few minutes he'd isolated a gold necklace, a silver and stone mosaic brooch and a gold charm bracelet. He then handed me $550 in crisp bills. I could not hide my surprise and delight. That put the Friends of Fieldworkers treasury back in positive territory!

I contacted the donor and told her Friends of Fieldworkers, Inc., would give a $2,000 college scholarship (through House Farmworkers!) and her gift would pay for 1/4 of that. She was very pleased.

Whether given as a gift to farmworkers or sold for cash, jewelry can be a lovely gift.

Car Donations

Our friends Christine (Ojai Apothecary) and Eric Hodge (Hodge Podge Garage) live around the corner and were some of our first new friends in Ojai five years ago. They have supported our efforts in many ways. Their daughters, Autumn and Amber, are also delightful friends who amaze us with their talents and varied interests. Autumn has helped me in the orchard and also with the chickens. She is a real chicken-whisperer.

One day, Eric called and asked if we'd be interested in a van that one of his customers wanted to donate. Would we ever! This Toyota Sienna seats seven people, but without the seats it can haul more than a small truck. It's carried hundreds of bags of clothes, toys, food, and boxes of food, books and household belongings. We have transported tables, chairs, book cases, single beds and other small pieces of furniture to families.

Another friend donated a well-cared-for Mercury Sable, and after we paid to have it registered and smogged, we sold it and made a nice profit for Friends of Fieldworkers.

Ted wrote letters to 35 individual car dealers in our county to see if they might be willing to donate a used car at year's end. He followed up with phone calls. So far, no one has responded. We'd love to be able to supply dependable, low-gas mileage cars to fieldworkers who need them.

Other fundraising ideas follow: We held GoFundMe Campaigns for the annual Payless Shoes Gift Card event where we raised approximately

$3,000. And $6,000 for the families in the fatal apartment fire. Approximately $600 in two birthday campaigns that paid for a teen's dental bills. As a nonprofit we discovered we were eligible for donations through the PayPal Giving Fund and Network for Good fund. The benefit of the latter is lower "processing fees" and immediate letters of thanks and donation receipts sent by them to donors.

The rest of the time we have relied on writing letters to our family, friends, acquaintances and yes, even strangers, asking for money to pay for whatever the current need is.

This means we presently have a rather short donor list. We may consider a crowdfunding system to keep our donors interested, informed and sending in money.

Getting the Word Out

Marketing your nonprofit takes time and creative ideas. The first thing you will want to create is your website. We set up our website with the help of GoDaddy, but other web hosting companies that come highly recommended are InMotion, Bluehost, HostGator, 1&1 IONOS, Tsohost, Wix, and Weebly.

Next, you will want to promote your activities through the use of social media. Having a marketing/social media person on your board, or at least as a regular volunteer, is highly recommended. Facebook, Snapchat, Instagram and Pinterest are the best social media sites to begin with. Getting your activities covered by your local newspaper is great for your nonprofit's visibility. Your marketing person should send press releases to local newspapers every time you have a special event or something important happens as a result of your work.

Service clubs like Rotary, Kiwanis, Lions, Optimists and Soroptimists are always looking for presenters at their regular meetings. It's best if you have a special project you are working on and are seeking support to make it a reality. Just Google the clubs in your local area and you will find contact information.

Churches are also good places to let people know of your presence in the community. Many churches have committees or groups dedicated to activities around community service, and many are looking for opportunities to hear about new organizations in their city or town.

Hooplaha is a national news service dedicated to good news only. We were fortunate to be featured on *Hooplaha* as a result of daughter Jennie's contacts in the local and national media. Google their name for contact information.

Recordkeeping

I want to keep a computer spread sheet of all families we serve—contact information, birthdays, clothing and shoe sizes, interests, ways we've supported them, favorite books and dreams. I keep random handwritten notes of this in binders but a digital record would be much more efficient and accessible. This I have not yet done. It's a great volunteer opportunity. One high school student created a calendar of birthdays and addresses of all our fieldworkers five years ago.

The purpose of this is to keep in touch with our friends, follow-up and match them up with donations and services as they become available.

Antidote for Fatigue

Being a peace and justice activist can be exhilarating and very rewarding. Sometimes it's exhausting. Most of the time the work itself fuels the effort. But sometimes I flat out get really tired: 1) tired of the physical labor of picking-up, cleaning, repairing and delivering items; 2) tired of the emotional energy required in working with poor people struggling to live day-to-day; and 3) tired of the misunderstanding of people who either don't understand our motivations or fundamentally disagree with what we are doing.

The clear signal to me of my own *compassion fatigue*, as some people call it, is when I feel bothered, interrupted, or irritated by a person's request. My general reaction is a positive, mobilized-for-action response. *Sure, I'll get right on it!* But when I feel annoyed at a person's response when I deliver what they asked for, or if I just don't have the energy to get up off the couch to tackle my next project, I now recognize the sign.

I have lived with GAD (Generalized Anxiety Disorder) which sometimes is accompanied by depression, since I was a young girl. This impacted every aspect of my life and made it difficult to stay in one job for more than a couple of years. The fact that I am still doing this work into our 7th year speaks of the good match for me. And every job I had as a parent, educator, salesperson, college student, and chaplain trainee prepared me for the work I do now. I love this work. But sometimes I get really tired.

Some antidotes are 1) reminding myself that what Friends of Fieldworkers does for people is a drop in the bucket and there are others out there doing other things for or with them. They will survive if we aren't here; 2) acknowledging that all friendships take time, effort and space; and 3) taking a break to have a change of pace: a few days of gardening, sewing, doing other art projects, writing or simply resting; 4) allowing our friends to come to us and do something for us and 5) making trips to our families in Cos Cob, Phoenix, Austin and Santa Monica.

One friend brought over chicken noodle and vegetable soup when I had a cold. One family came over after the St. Thomas fire to see if we were really okay. We had a lovely visit and chatted in the living room, snacking on Hawaiian chocolate-covered macadamia nuts and fresh-squeezed orange juice. The three children interpreted, and it was a very lovely visit.

Sometimes, this fatigue is relieved by talking to someone else who also loves other people in distress and loves to give. "Motherpod" helps me gain perspective and feel better by just talking with me. And the same is for my husband who also cares deeply for fieldworkers but somehow (temperament or training?) remains distant enough not to burn out.

Another way is to learn to delegate. In 2019 we have some new ways to reach fieldworkers...to support the systems and programs in place.

We gave $2,000 to House Farm Workers! the nonprofit that addresses housing needs of fieldworkers and awards three or four $2,000 college scholarships annually, to deserving students of fieldworkers.

We gave another $2,000 to the Ventura County Pediatric Diagnostic Clinic through their foundation, Landon Pediatric Foundation, to meet emergency needs of farmer families whose children are sick or injured and need some support. They can use these funds at their discretion.

Another $3,500 will be given as a scholarship to the Encampment for Citizenship for this year's nearly month-long conference to be held on the campus of California State University Channel Islands in Camarillo, California, about 32 miles from Ojai, our headquarters.

Approximately $2,000 will go for one young woman's orthodontia and another $3,000 for the Annual Shoe Gift Card event. A gift from Marty McMillan, an Ojai supporter, were the proceeds from her yard sale. These were given to a local organization's annual backpack and school supply drive. These are the basics.

Opportunities for Volunteers

Many people see our website (www.friendsoffieldworkers.org), our Facebook page of the same name, or our U-Tube clip at http://bit.ly/2mpuU8A (by Hooplaha—thank you for the introduction, Jennie). They get inspired and want to help.

They call or email us. I send them a list of jobs for volunteers and that's the last time I hear from them. We really have needed a volunteer organizer.

Here's a partial list of jobs for volunteers:

1- Social Media (Facebook, website, Twitter, Snap Chat)
2- Data Base Management (Secretarial aid/ computer person)
3- Communications, Public Relations spokesperson (with newspaper, magazines and other media)
4- In-kind donations requester/handler (furniture, cars, household items, clothing)
5- Bookkeeper
6- Speaker's Bureau
7- Professional Resources (legal, health, dental, education, immigration,)
8- Board Member
9- Interpreter/Translator (FOF newsletters and mail to fieldworkers, rental agreement forms, banking forms)
10- Community Partnership Coordinator
11- Historian/Researcher/Archivist (check newpapers/media for articles, farmworker news)
12- Librarian (collect books about fieldworkers, Oaxaca, Mexico, and farming for a CSUCI library collection)
13- Family Contact Person (needs coordinator; regular caller/ updater of family information/requests
14- Liaison with Local Farmers and their workforce managers
15- Clothing (wash, sort and make minor repairs, and distribute)
16- Hospitality (friendly visits, hot meals)
17- Fundraiser (grant writer, big events planner)

18- Special Services (Queen for a day; massage, hair and skin care, garden-in-a-box, libraries-in-a-box, "Blankies & Books" with schools, tutors)

19- Birthday card + $5/ or $10/adult (approx. 50 cards total per year)

20- Church representative

21- Speakers' Bureau (Lions, Rotary, other service clubs)

22- Liaison with *Food Forward* (possibly, *Food Share)*

23- Truck Driver and Storage/delivery

24- Court accompanist (when a fieldworker goes to court)

25- writer/blogger about life of fieldworkers

26- fieldworker presence/visibility (acquisition of Giant Roadside Art Murals of Fieldworkers by Salinas artist, John Cerney)

PART III

A DREAM FOR DREAMERS

Writing things down has a miraculous way of making them come true. For that reason I am going to write a scenario of what I dream for all fieldworkers everywhere, again using the framework of Maslow's Pyramid of Needs.

This is a story about Victor and Alejandra, two fieldworkers who came across the Mexican-American Border into California with the blessing of both governments. They came on a comfortable bus provided by the Mexican-American Transit System, with introductory work papers from the American Immigration Board. They were met in San Diego by representatives of *Farmers United*, an organized group of agricultural companies in need of hard-working and loyal workers on their farms. They had a personal greeter-rep who welcomed them to America. There were even people clapping for them as they moved through the entrance.

Victor and Alejandra are a young couple wanting to create a life in America where they and their future children can reach their highest potential. They are from Oaxaca and speak Mixtec. There are interpreters who meet them, with the farm representatives. Together they fill out a form that describes the type of fruit or vegetables they are interested in working with; whether in the fields, nursery or cannery. It is explained that if they learn the English language and take advantage of other educational offerings, they will have opportunities to seek other jobs in agriculture or eventually, in other areas.

They are asked what they did in their homeland? What interests, skills, or other activities were they involved in? This can help farmers decide where they would be the most skilled and satisfied in their work.

Alejandra and Victor are asked if they want to stay put in one town or move around the state with their favorite crops. What are their plans—to stay and earn enough money to return to their homeland or to live permanently in the United States? Of course, this plan may change depending of their life experiences.

What type of weather conditions do they prefer? California has agriculture of all kinds in all types of weather.

Based on their answers, Victor and Alejandra will meet two or three farm representatives who tell them about their own farm's specific offerings. They must be truthful because there are regular farm visits by an impartial team of quality assurance-type people to make sure the farm keeps its promises to the fieldworkers. If they do not, there are consequences. They comply or they are dropped by Farmers United which will be economically devastating.

After Victor and Alejandra decide which two locations they'd like to visit, a tour is arranged. After that, there is an introductory year where they have a chance to work together. After that year, for any reason, they may try a new location.

Farmers know that it is a solid social, psychological and economical choice to treat their fieldworkers with respect, fairness, honesty and compassion. It costs a great deal of money to recruit and train new workers.

Victor and Alejandra are provided with a healthy, reasonable, well-designed and maintained, well-lit, single-family bungalow. They start paying rent, one-quarter of their income, a month after they arrive so they have a chance to earn it. Solar and wind power are used to provide them with fresh and filtered water, efficient heat and cooling. A stove, refrigerator, microwave are provided with instructions on how to use them safely.

Their home is one of twenty, surrounded by beautiful trees, flowers and a community garden which is a meeting place for families and a source for their choice of vegetables, fruit and herbs. It contains a composting system for their kitchen waste and a garden supervisor.

There are several thrift stores within walking distance that have clothing, shoes, housewares, beds, linen and small appliances. And there are grocery stores with locally-grown organic produce. The farm provides them with a generous allowance for food and other household supplies the first two months, allowing them time to adjust to this new, foreign environment.

Victor & Alejandra will be introduced to the older "tenants" in a welcome meal. They also will be assigned a farm representative to talk to with any questions or personal problems such as illness or death in their family back home. There will be a satisfaction foreman to address job-related issues without fear of reprisal. An interpreter will be provided.

Because they have work permission papers, Victor & Alejandra will feel free to explore their new town on the United States, without constant fear of being "found out" and "returned". Because they can sleep safely, they will perform better at their jobs, miss less work and have fewer accidents.

Victor chooses to work in the strawberry fields because he has a strong back and had some experience with that at home. Alejandra chooses the nursery because she loves planting and caring for flowers and young vegetables.

The regular work schedule is five days/week. The sixth day is for taking classes in English, farm-related topics, cultural and health-related workshops in banking, time-management, family-planning, nutrition, etc. Specially-trained fieldworker doctors, dentists, bankers, and other professionals will be available on the 6th day for appointments. Shuttle rides are provided. Late afternoon or evening appointments during the week may also be provided to avoid missed work and long hours in an emergency room.

A special credit union will meet clients as soon as they join the farm and explain all the benefits. Victor and Alejandra are surprised by all the things they can do though this company—start their membership with only $5, have their salaries direct-deposited or cashed with no charge and enable them to send money home to their parents or other family in Mexico with no change.

Salaries are about 20% above minimum wage plus there are incentives for them to earn more, based on the quality and dependability of their work.

The farm provides a retirement program that they will contribute to, along with their taxes. At the retirement age of 64, they will be eligible to retire since they will also have been paying into Social Security and will be eligible for Medicare. Some families decide to return home to Mexico where they have been building a home and where their savings and retirement will go much farther. If they decide to return, their children may continue to stay if they pursue higher education and are then gainfully employed.

Who pays for this professional care? CaliCare, an insurance company owned and administered by Farmers United and paid for by a tax charged on all fruit, vegetables, and other produce and commodities provided by fieldworkers. Also, any companies using unfair labor practices, or unsafe chemicals that impact any of California's citizens or environment, will be charged large fines and shut down if they don't comply.

Consumers will also pay about 23% more for produce. However, this will be saved on their health bills, now that pesticides are stringently managed and limited to only organic ones.

Other organizations such as community service groups, churches, political activism clubs and nonprofits such as Friends of Fieldworkers, Inc., will be encouraged to reach out to Alejandra and Victor, to welcome them to the community.

They will notice immediately, that the children in their neighborhood are well-fed, healthy, and well-cared for. Their parents have part of one day and all day Sunday to take them to the parks in the neighborhood, the zoo, the beach, to church, shopping or to relax at home.

If Alejandra and Victor decide to start their own family sometime, they will have some healthy options, such as birthing, nutrition and parenting classes, and Alejandra can reduce her work load, change the site or stop entirely if she needs to do so for a healthy pregnancy. She gets 6-weeks paid maternity leave. He gets paid paternity leave for 4-weeks. There are nearly zero mother and baby deaths. There is a special family stipend when either of them opts for permanent birth control, covered by their insurance.

And, there is a state-of-the-art bilingual Montessori Day Care, Preschool and Elementary school in the neighborhood provided free to fieldworkers. It is maintained and operated in cooperation with the local university's department of early childhood education. Parents are released from work to attend parent-conferences. There are reading and math incentives for children and special education resources, if needed.

There are reduced-price coin laundries in each group of twenty bungalows. Solar powered washing and drying machines are designed to conserve water, safely wash and disinfect heavily soiled clothes, even muddy work clothes and diapers. A state-of-the-art diaper service is available to families who choose cloth diapers at half the price of paper diapers.

Very affordable and safe babysitting services are available to parents who need time alone or time to get things done without their children. There are also childcare banking co-ops which allow parents to exchange care within their group of new friends and neighbors.

Victor and Alejandra are encouraged to use as many as they can of the services offered in this farm-life program. And to take classes through the local school district or Agricultural Farm Board. They are reminded of their value as providers of California's and America's food. And also encouraged to reach their highest potential in life, even if that means leaving their farm for a different occupation.

There are other classes in adult basic education, agri-business and management, plumbing, construction, hospitality, restaurant, computer, and other industries, should they wish to transfer into other fields. These are offered in the local community colleges in the evenings and during their two-month paid vacations.

At the end of their first full day in their new home, Alejandra and Victor notice a group of men and women playing volleyball on the dirt volleyball court outside their house. They seem to be from many different backgrounds. Is it possible that other countries provide fieldworkers to California? Or that Americans actually choose to work here? This farm takes farming to a new level. Or maybe this is what it used to be.

PART IV

DREAMS FOR FRIENDS OF FIELDWORKERS, INC. BY 2024

Board of Directors:

There will be a board of seven members. They will be the following: President, Vice President/Volunteer Coordinator, Secretary, Treasurer, Fundraiser, Community Liaison, and Education Advocate.

The **President** will oversee and support the six other members of the Board and their responsibilities, and make sure there are at least quarterly meetings and more if necessary. She/He will review the FOF Mission and revise it if at least 5/7 members agree. The only phrase that must always be included is that FOF "is to befriend and support fieldworkers." By-Laws will be established to fit and support the Mission. All ideas from the board members will be considered and voted upon. Any idea that fits the mission and by-laws of FOF will be acted upon with a 5/7 vote.

The **Vice President** will work closely with the President. and be the volunteer coordinator.

The **Secretary** will be very familiar with writing business letters, and thank you letters once the money/donations are recorded by the Treasurer.

The **Treasurer** will be a certified accountant and file the annual tax report. She/he will keep a spreadsheet of all the money/donations to FOF and all the expenditures for the needs of fieldworkers. And will give an updated report at each meeting.

The **Fundraiser,** an experienced grant writer and event planner, will seek grants that fit the activities and goals of FOF. She/He will write the grant with input from the appropriate board member(s) or if there is funding, pay someone to help.

The **Community Liaison** will stay in regular, frequent contact with FOF's Community partners and seek ways to collaborate or to support their activities that are for fieldworkers. He/She will be in charge of adding members to our Professional Pool of medical and dental specialists, attorneys (immigration, workforce, landlord issues, medical malpractice), tutors, education therapists, etc.

The **Education Advocate** will work closely with the families whose children have education funds in the V.C. Credit Union. When their semester grades come out, she/he will review them and send a notice to the treasurer of how much money to deposit in their account or to send them a check directly for them to deposit. She/He may arrange a phone or in-person appointment with the children's teachers throughout the year to make sure they are on-track and have what they need to succeed. They may require an interpreter.

The following services will be available for fieldworkers:

1) Childcare facilities in various part of Ventura county.
2) A board of advocacy fieldworkers may contact with any issues and expect helpful/reciprocal responses.
3) A Grameen-type bank specifically for all their banking needs.
4) A Housing Authority that helps people find good, adequate housing.

A tax will exist on all businesses in the county that rely on the services and work of fieldworkers that will pay for affordable and safe housing. Closer watch over landlords will prevent price-gouging, frequent electrical fires, over-crowding, rodent-infestation, fear of reprisal for legitimate complaints such as repair of leaks, broken appliances, non-working heaters, etc.

5) Educational programs similar to First Five, Head Start, Tri-Counties and Educational Therapy Alliance that specifically cater to the most vulnerable of our children. Pay now or pay for incarceration and MediCal and disability benefits later.

6) One-stop Shop legal, educational, social, medical centers around the county will provide accessible services.

7) Immigration reform or state-wide underground (alternative) accommodations will occur including SNAP (Supplemental Nutrition Assistance Program) disability, medical and life insurance; paid maternity, sick and vacation leave. A retirement plan will be available to them if they worked and paid taxes in California for more than a certain time.

8) Stores, similar to Walmart, that are more politically, morally and economically responsible.

9) Fresh, healthy, and affordable fruit, vegetables and other foods are available throughout the county.

10) Clinics that provide regular well-baby/child check-ups with dental, vision and hearing screening at times that parents are available and as much as possible with simultaneous scheduling so that they don't have to take off work more than necessary.

Birth control methods will regularly be explained, available, and encouraged, especially before the birth of a fourth child. Voluntary sterilization will be compensated after a period of counseling and time for reflection.

The most progressive employers build in paid leave for these medical appointments so that their agricultural operations are not affected.

11) State-wide emergency communications are universal, and not only in English, such as was the case in the recent Thomas Fires: warnings to evacuate and news about the progress of the

fire are in Spanish, Mixtec, Tagalog and other major languages of California.

12) It is illegal for employees to be forced to work in the fields in unfavorable conditions such as severe heat, cold, storm, and fire events.

Heavy penalties will be charged on the companies that penalize their workers for leaving these unsafe conditions. AND, the agricultural companies will be granted stipends or other government support during such events.

13) Although produce prices are somewhat higher, our citizens are willing to pay, in lieu of having a total shut-down of farming due to lack of farmworkers.

14) Through the public library system, fieldworkers' stories will be welcomed, recorded and printed for children and adults, and circulated to increase understanding, empathy and appreciation.

15) Summer camps, preferably outdoors in the mountains, beach or other natural areas, will be available to all fieldworker children during the summer and other vacations to avoid being behind locked doors in an apartment with a babysitter all summer.

16) Working with the county and cities, there will be an explosion in the number of community gardens and playgrounds, particularly in high-crime areas. Community centers that supply a myriad supervised activities to children and teens will give them a safe place to be and to use their energy. In these there will be volunteer and paid work opportunities for children as young as 11.

17) Friends of Fieldworkers, Inc., will have a seat on the City Councils of every town. And it will work with other organizations like CLUE, CAUSE, and Rotary and Lions to raise awareness and funds.

18) An endowed scholarship at CSU Channel Islands, Ventura, Moorpark and Oxnard Community Colleges will be in place for all qualified fieldworker children, if not for tuition, at least for books, fees and other expenses.

19) For students who attend other schools of higher learning (including vocational schools, art, medical, industrial arts, etc.,) there will also be a special compensation for them similar to the Peace Corps or AmeriCorps.

20) A state-of-the-art training center will be available to students who are more inclined to work with their hands and creative side of their brain—in music and the visual arts; auto, truck or airplane mechanics; culinary or visual arts. For those who prefer to work with children or adults in other capacities, there will be certified training for this as well.

21) John Cerney's farm art will appear all over the county, on every major farm land, depicting the people who feed us through their back-breaking effort. This will raise awareness and appreciation and the personal esteem of farm workers everywhere.

PART V

BIBLIOGRAPHY

Lists of Books

Popular Migrant Farmworkers Books (36)
https://www.goodreads.com/shelf/show/migrant-farmworkers

Migrant Farmworker Families: Books for Kids (annotated)
http://www.colorincolorado.org/booklist/migrant-farmworker-families-books-kids

¡Colorin colorado! A bilingual site for educators and families of English language learners. Books are listed in the categories of Young Children, Kids, Young Adults, Educators, Immigration Stories: Crossing the Border, etc.
colorincolorado.org

Videos, Movies

The Harvest (La Cosecha), Directed by U. Roberto Romano;
A 2010 documentary film about agricultural child labor in America.
https://www.imdb.com/title/tt1981703

This Angel Helps Immigrant Field Workers, This Hooplaha original video was produced by Tracy Chevrier and shot by Alex   Simon and edited by Kellie Sieban. For Only Good TV. http://bit.ly/2mpuU8A

Further Reading:

Bowe, John. *Nobodies: Modern American Slave Labor and the Dark Side of the New Global Economy*, Random House, 2007.

Buffini, Brian. *The Emigrant Edge: How to Make It Big in America.* New York, Howard Books, 2017.

Calvita, Kitty, *Inside the State: The Bracero Program, Immigration, and the I.N.S. (After the Law)*, United Kingdom, 1993.

Cohen, Deborah, *Braceros: Migrant Citizens and Transnational Subjects in the Postwar United States and Mexico*, Chapel Hill, The University of North Carolina Press, 2011.

Estabrook, Barry. *Tomatoland: How Modern Industrial Agriculture Destroyed Our Most Alluring Fruit*, Andrew McMeel Publishing, 2011.

Grande, Reyna. *Across A Hundred Mountains*. New York, Atria Books, 2006.

Hellman, Judith Adler. *The World of Mexican Migrants: The Rock and the Hard Place*. New York, The New Press, 2008.

Holmes, Seth, *Fresh Fruit, Broken Bodies: Migrant Farmworkers in the United States*, University of California Press, May 2013.

Jimenez, Francisco: *The Circuit: Stories from the life of a migrant child*, Houghton Mifflin Co. 1997.

Levy, Janey. *Illegal Immigration and Amnesty: Open Borders and National Security. New York, Rosen Publishing, 2010.*

Mize, Ronald L., *The Invisible Workers of the U.S.–Mexico Bracero Program: Obredos Olvidados.* United States, 2016.

Mize, Ronald and Alicia Swords, *Consuming Mexican Labor: From the Bracero Program to NAFTA,* University of Toronto, 2011.

Perez, Amada Irma, Maya Christina Gonzalez. *My Very Own Room.* Children's Book Press, May 2000.

Ramirez, Florencia. *Eat Less Water.* Red Hen Press, 2017.

Web Sites and Articles:

¡Colorin colorado! A bilingual site for educators and families of English Language learners
https://www.colorincolorado.org

Center for Farmworker Families: Education, Advocacy and Support: Recommended Books and Movies
http://www.farmworkerfamily.org/recommended-reading

Center for Farmworker Families: Education, Advocacy and Support
http://www.farmworkerfamily.org/information

CRB: *Farmworkers in California: A Brief Introductions*, October, 2013.
https://latinocaucus.legislature.ca.gov/sites/latinocaucus.legislature.ca.gov/files/CRB%20Report%20on%20Farmworkers%20in%20CA%20S-13-017.pdf

Guidi, Ruxandra. Farmworkers face illness and death in the fields, *High Country News*, August, 2018.
https://www.hcn.org/issues/50.14/agriculture-californias-farmworkers-face-illness-and-death-in-the-fields

Rights of Farmworkers in California, *La Cooperativa Campesina de California*
http://www.lacooperativa.org/rights-farmworkers-california-3/

Wages rise on California farms. Americans still don't want the job. by Natalie Kitroef and Gregory Mohan, *L.A. Times, Stockton*, March, 2017
https://www.latimes.com/projects/la-fi-farms-immigration/

Guest column: Central Valley field workers strive for better lives, Livier Martinez and Victoria Rocha, *Visalia Times Delta*, October, 2018.
https://www.visaliatimesdelta.com/story/opinion/2018/10/19/guest-column-central-valley-field-workers-strive-better-lives/1685888002/

California's undocumented workers help the economy grow—but may pay the cost, by Valerie Hamilton, *P.R.I.'s The World*, March, 2017.
https://www.pri.org/stories/2017-03-06/californias-undocumented-workers-help-grow-economy-theres-cost

Helping Hands: Nonprofit helps undocumented immigrants, Tyler Hersko, *Ventura County Star,* April, 2017.
https://www.vcstar.com/story/money/business/2017/04/13/nonprofit-connects-undocumented-immigrants-community/98805522/

Helping all farmworkers (Opinion by Ted Lucas), *Ventura County Star*, April, 2017.
https://www.vcstar.com/story/opinion/readers/2017/04/18/helping-all-farmworkers/100629680/

This Angel Helps Immigrant Field Workers Live a Better Life! *Huffpost,* Hooplaha–Only Good News, Contributor, February, 2017.
https://www.huffpost.com/entry/this-angel-helps-immigrant-field-workers-live-a-better_b_58b5a394e4b02f3f81e44c93

A New Generation: 7 Inspiring Immigration Stories, by Carmen Ballon, *Only Good TV*
https://www.onlygood.tv/a-new-generation-7-inspiring-immigration-stories-2465358389.html

http://toronto.nooneisillegal.org

Center for Immigration Studies
https://cis.org

U.S. Citizenship and Immigration Services
https://www.uscis.gov

National Network for Immigrant and Refugee Rights
http://www.nnirr.org

National Farmworker Ministry
http://nfwm.org

PART VI

THANK YOU'S

Businesses

Barclay's Insurance, Oxnard
Christians Acting Together Store (CATS), Camarillo
Morgan Thrift Store, Oak View
New 2 You Thrift Store, Ojai
Oxnard Rescue Mission Super Thrift, Oxnard
Second Helpings Thrift, Ojai

Churches & Service Organizations

Abundant Table
ACTION (Area Christians Taking Initiative on Needs)
All Saints Episcopal Church, Oxnard
Camarillo Amber's Light Lions Club奐
Dem-Moms of Camarillo
Mount Cross Lutheran Church, Camarillo
Outlaw Quilters, Port Hueneme
North Oxnard United Methodist Church, Oxnard
Social Justice Fund for Ventura County
St. Jude's Catholic Church, (Loaves & Fishes), Westlake Village

Two Trees Community Church, Ventura
Unitarian Universalist Church of Ventura

Farms/Farmers

Abundant Table/Join the Farm
Brokaw, Ellen and Norma
Deardorff Family Farms
DeBusschere-Morris, Paul & Julie

Medical/Dental Groups

Dr. Christoph Haar, orthodontist, Ojai/Ventura
Dr. Robert Jordan, dermatologist/Ventura
Dr. David Neumeister, Vista Pacific Dental Care/Oxnard
Dr. Mahtab Partovi, 360 Orthodontics/Los Angeles
Dr. Josephine Soliz, family medicine/Oxnard
Dr. Greg Wolfe, dentist/Ventura

Legal Groups

Antonio Flores, California Rural Legal Assistance, Inc. (CRLA)/
Oxnard
Vanessa Frank, Immigration Attorney/Ventura
Gabriela Navarro-Busch, Immigration Attorney, Ventura

Individuals (for largest or most frequent gifts in kind, time or cash)

Darla Drain
Aiesha Eleusizov
Margo (Susan) Geiger
Dr. Christoph Haar
B.L. Hernandez

Christine and Eric Hodge
Martita Martinez-Bravo
Mark & Marvelle Karahadian
Jennie O'Hagan Korneychuk
KuanFen and Terilyn Liu
Motherpod & Family
Julie Morris
Suzie Nixon
Vern Novstrup
Tim O'Hagan
Alexis O'Neill & Barbara Veazey
Roanna Prell
Alma Ramirez
Craig Rosen
Robert and Marilyn Salas
Ellen Sklars
Lorelei O'Hagan Strange
Jackie and John Treuting

EVERY gift of time, means and love is appreciated beyond words.

INDEX

AUTHOR AND EDITOR

Judy Fisk Lucas is a haole with a Hawaiian heart, having grown up in Waimea, Kauai and Kona, Hawaii. Her parents were missionaries with The Hawaiian Church and the Foreign Church in Waimea and the first Christian Church in Hawaii, Mokuaikaua Church, in Kailua-Kona plus six others along the Kona Coast.

She attended colleges in Santa Rosa, Santa Barbara, San Jose and Camarillo, California, as well as Albuquerque, New Mexico. She taught school for many years–migrant, inner city, elementary, middle, high, ESL and adult education. She worked in business for Zellerbach and Prudential and with her first husband, Kim O'Hagan, raised three children, Jennie, Lorelei and Tim. Other ventures have included educational therapy, hospital chaplaincy, children's literature, master gardening and grandparenting long distance.

Working with fieldworkers throughout her life and especially in the past seven years, has given her many opportunities to befriend, love, share, nurture, listen to, care for and learn from them. She has done so with the love and support of her husband, Ted.

She and Ted, their poodle mixes, Wiley and Willow, share a home in Ojai with six hens and a very forgiving betta fish, *Patience.*

Theodore Drexel Lucas (Ted) grew up in El Cajon, California, after living in Texas, Washington, and Pennsylvania for brief periods of time while his father was in the Navy. He attended El Cajon Valley High School and after graduation attended San Diego State University, where he got his B.A. and M.A. degrees in music.

Following his graduation from SDSU, he was accepted as a student of Mlle. Nadia Boulanger, and spent a year in Paris, France, studying composition with her. While in Paris, he was accepted as a graduate student in composition at the University of Illinois, where he completed his doctorate in composition and ethnomusicology.

He taught music briefly at the University of Missouri and at Beloit College before becoming chairman of the music department at Beloit. From there, his career took him into administrative positions at Southwestern University in Texas, San Jose State University, and finally CSU Channel Islands, in Camarillo, California, where he served as Provost and Vice President for Academic Affairs.

He has since retired from the university and devotes his time to composing music, playing violin and viola in string quartets, serving as Minister of Music at an Episcopal Church, and helping Judy with the charity they founded, Friends of Fieldworkers, Inc., by serving as treasurer. Its mission is to befriend and serve those who provide our food.

Contact Friends of Fieldworkers, Inc.
Judy and Ted Lucas
805 312-0579
judy.fisk.lucas@gmail.com
ted.lucas@csuci.edu
P.O. Box 1166
Oak View, CA 93022

Accuracy is our goal. If there are errors or omissions, please contact us and we will correct the next printing.

CPSIA information can be obtained
at www.ICGtesting.com
Printed in the USA
FSHW012023301119
64521FS

Photo by Donna Granata,
www.FocusOnTheMasters.com

Photo by Jennie O'Hagan
www.Jennieomedia.com

Friends of Fieldworkers: True Personal stories of triumph, tears and invisibility. A Chronicle of Love is the history of the creation and work of a non profit charity devoted to befriending and helping fieldworkers and their families of Ventura County.

Judy Fisk Lucas was born in San Francisco and raised in Hawaii. She moved to Ventura Co. following her marriage to Ted Lucas in 1999. Her three children live with their families in California, Arizona and Connecticut. Her bonus children and their families live in Texas. She co-founded FoF after retiring from her education/business career.

Theodore Drexel Lucas (Ted) grew up in San Diego, son of a naval officer and a farmer's daughter. His three sons and their families all live in the Austin, Texas area. He is the founding Provost of CSU Channel Islands and the co-founder of FoF. As a music composer, he has several published compositions.

Roxie Ray was born and raised in Orange County, California. She moved to Ventura County in 1983 and began to study art around 1990. Ray is known for her fieldworker paintings and anatomical figures in water. Her style can be described as Expressionistic. In her own words, *She was drawn to portray and create a closer look at the anonymous, yet strangely familiar view of the marginalized farmworker population.*

Maslow's Pyramid of Basic Needs

Xlibris

A TEENAGER'S GUIDE TO FINDING THEIR TRUE CALLING

THROAT PUNCH NORMAL

JOE ELLIOTT
WITH ZAC TINNEY